THE MEATLESS COOKBOOK

LILLIAN SMIT

THE MEATLESS COOKBOOK

ROBERT HALE & COMPANY

LONDON

2?1

First published in Great Britain 1975

ISBN 0 7091 5369 4

Printed by Citadel Press, Lansdowne, Cape

CONTENTS

METRICAL TABLE
(To nearest gram)

1 oz =　28 grams

2 oz =　57 grams

4 oz = 113 grams

6 oz = 170 grams

8 oz = 227 grams

10 oz = 283 grams

12 oz = 340 grams

14 oz = 396 grams

16 oz or 1 lb = 454 grams

1 oz = 3 level tablespoons dry breadcrumbs

1 oz = 5 level tablespoons fresh breadcrumbs

1 oz = 4 level tablespoons grated raw carrots and
other root vegetables

1 oz = 4 level tablespoons grated cheese

1 oz = 4 level tablespoons maizena

1 oz = 3 level tablespoons flour

1 oz = 1 level tablespoon butter, margarine

1 oz = 2 level tablespoons raisins

1 oz = 1 level tablespoon dry lentils, peas

1 oz = 2 level tablespoons oil

1 oz = 1 level tablespoon rice

1 oz = 2 level tablespoons sugar

1 oz = 1 level tablespoon grated nuts

INTRODUCTION

Cooking has such variety that it can be seen as an art greatly able to please those fortunate enough to be the recipients of careful, good and creative cooking.

The recipes in this book I have collected over more years than I like to remember. Those put together here will provide protein value as good as and, in my opinion, better from a health point of view, than that obtained from meat.

If I can help in this respect as well as providing some recipes easier on the pocket than very expensive meat, I shall be delighted.

Recipes can be protein enriched with special ingredients such as skim milk (dry or liquid); flour can be substituted with whole wheat or soya flour; white sugar with brown or treacle sugar. Many supermarkets have a health centre which supplies nutritious ingredients.

Most of the recipes are for 2–3 people. The exceptions will be numbered.

LILLIAN SMIT

BAKED LOAVES

1. ASPARAGUS LOAF BAKE

1 cup cracker crumbs
½ cup hot milk
1 tin asparagus cuts
1 beaten egg
Savoury white sauce
2 tablespoons margarine or oil
½ chopped onion
Chopped parsley or celery leaves
Seasoning

Combine the ingredients except the white sauce. Place the mixture in a greased loaf tin and bake till set in a moderate oven. Serve with sauce.

Savoury white sauce
1 tablespoon flour or maizena
1 tablespoon margarine or butter
2 cups milk or half milk, half stock
½ tablespoon margarine
¼ cup chopped olives
Seasoning

Melt the margarine and blend in the flour. Gradually add the milk and stir till smooth. Add the margarine, olives, seasoning.

2. Bean Loaf

1 cup cooked mashed beans
½ cup grated cheese
½ cup breadcrumbs
¼ cup milk
2 tablespoons chopped onion
1 tablespoon chopped parsley
2 beaten eggs
½ tablespoons dry mustard
Seasoning
Oil

Combine the ingredients and place the mixture in a greased loaf tin. Bake 20 to 30 minutes in a moderate oven.

3. Cashew Nut Loaf

2 thick slices trimmed brown bread
½ cup chopped cashew nuts
¼ cup other chopped nuts
¼ cup oil
113 grams sliced raw or tinned mushrooms
A little vegetable stock
½ sliced onion
1 tablespoon margarine
1 beaten egg
½ dessertspoon chopped parsley
Paprika
Salt

Soak the bread in the stock and add the rest of the ingredients except the margarine. Place the mixture in a greased loaf tin. Dot with margarine and bake for 20 to 30 minutes in a moderate oven.

4. Cheese and Walnut Loaf

1½–2 cups flour
½ cup grated cheddar
¾ cup chopped walnuts
¾–1 cup top milk
2 beaten eggs
2 tablespoons margarine
2 teaspoons baking powder
1 teaspoon dry mustard
Seasoning

Sift flour, baking powder, seasoning, mustard. Grate and rub in the margarine till the mixture is crumby. Add the cheese, nuts and combined eggs and milk for a soft dough that will drop easily from a spoon. Place it in a greased loaf tin. Bake about 40 minutes in a 375°F. oven.

(*3–4 people*)

5. Cream Cheese Loaf

1 cup cream cheese
½ cup chopped peanuts
1 cup milk
1 cup cold cooked oatmeal
1 tablespoon chopped onion
1 tablespoon margarine (melted)
2 beaten eggs
½ teaspoon Worcester sauce
Seasoning

In a greased loaf tin place the combined ingredients. Bake 30–40 minutes in a moderate oven.

(*3–4 people*)

6. Nut and Egg Loaf

$3\frac{1}{2}$–4 cups stale breadcrumbs
$\frac{1}{2}$ cup chopped almonds or other nuts
$\frac{1}{4}$ cup light cream or Ideal milk
4 chopped hard eggs
2 raw beaten eggs
1 dessertspoon chopped onion
2 tablespoons tomato juice
1 teaspoon thyme
2 teaspoons celery salt
Seasoning

Combine the ingredients, adding enough tomato juice for a soft mixture. Place it in a greased loaf tin and bake till set. Serve with gravy.
(*4–5 people*)

7. Nut and Potato Loaf

$\frac{1}{4}$ cup mashed potato
$\frac{1}{2}$ cup chopped peanuts
$\frac{1}{2}$ cup breadcrumbs
1 beaten egg
2 tablespoons hot milk
2 tablespoons grated cheddar
1 tablespoon chopped onion
1 tablespoon melted margarine
$\frac{1}{2}$ teaspoon marmite

Soak the breadcrumbs in the combined hot milk and marmite. Add the rest of the ingredients and place the mixture in a greased loaf tin. Bake 25–30 minutes in a moderate oven. N.B. This mixture may also be shaped into a roast, be dotted with margarine and baked till set in a moderate oven. The ingredients may be doubled if a larger loaf or roast is wanted.

8. Peanut Butter and Carrot Loaf

2 thick slices trimmed bread
1 cup cooked chopped carrots
1 cup cooked mashed peas
1 tablespoon smooth peanut butter
1 tablespoon tomato sauce
1 beaten egg
Milk
Seasoning

Place the bread in a bowl and just cover it with milk. Let it soak for 5 minutes and then mash it. Add the rest of the ingredients and place the mixture in a greased loaf tin. Bake $\frac{1}{2}$ hour in a moderate oven.
(*3–4 people*)

9. Rice and Potato Loaf

1 cup cooked rice
$\frac{3}{4}$ cup cooked mashed potato
4 tablespoons breadcrumbs
2 tablespoons melted margarine
2 large beaten eggs
A little milk
1 large chopped onion
2 teaspoons chopped parsley
$\frac{1}{2}$ teaspoon grated lemon rind
Paprika
Seasoning

Combine all the ingredients except the margarine and place the mixture in a greased loaf tin. Pour the margarine over and bake 30–40 minutes in a moderate oven. Serve with gravy.

10. Spinach Loaf

1½ cups cooked chopped spinach
1 cup skinned dry-cooked tomato
½ cup cream cheese
2 beaten eggs
1 tablespoon melted margarine
3 tablespoons breadcrumbs
1 dessertspoon chopped onion
1 teaspoon marmite
½ teaspoon sugar
Seasoning
A little milk if needed

Combine the ingredients and place the mixture in a greased loaf tin. Bake till set in a moderate oven.

11. Walnut Loaf

1½ cups breadcrumbs
¾ cup chopped walnuts
¾–1 cup top milk
1 skinned chopped tomato
1 chopped onion
2 beaten eggs
1 tablespoon margarine
2 teaspoons baking powder
½ teaspoon mixed herbs
½ teaspoon sugar
Seasoning

Sprinkle the tomato with the sugar and fry it and the onion till they are soft. Remove the pan from the heat and add the crumbs, baking powder, walnuts, and mix. Add the combined eggs and top milk and place the mixture in a greased loaf tin. Bake till set in a moderate oven. N.B. A dash of curry powder may be added if wished. Serve with gravy.

MEATLESS ROASTS

1. ALMOND ROAST

2 thick trimmed slices brown bread
¾ cup chopped almonds or other nuts
½ cup warm soup
1 beaten egg
½ chopped onion
Oil
2 tablespoons melted margarine
½ teaspoon mixed herbs
Coating
Seasoning

Combine the soup and margarine and pour it over the bread. Let it soak for 5 minutes. Then mash it and add the rest of the ingredients except the coating. Make a roast of the mixture and place it on wax paper covered with a layer of coating. Gently press it all over with the coating so that it adheres. Then place it on a well-greased oven dish and bake it 30–40 minutes, basting it with oil at times.

Coating
2 tablespoons Kellog's bran
2 tablespoons dry breadcrumbs
2 tablespoons chopped nuts
Seasoning

Combine the ingredients and spread mixture on wax paper.

2. BEAN AND CARROT ROAST

227 grams soaked cooked dried beans
$\frac{1}{2}$ cup bean water
1 cup milk
$\frac{1}{2}$ cup grated carrots
$\frac{1}{2}$ cup breadcrumbs
2 teaspoons chopped parsley
$\frac{1}{4}$ teaspoon nutmeg
37–38 grams flour
37–38 grams margatine
37–38 grams oat meal or crushed Post Toasties
12 grams nut butter
Seasoning

Make a white sauce with the blended flour and margarine and the gradually added milk, stirring till smooth. Add the bean water and the combined mashed and sieved beans, the oatmeal, carrot, parsley, nutmeg, seasoning. With floured hands shape a roast and place it on a greased oven sheet which has been sprinkled with a layer of breadcrumbs. Dot the roast with margarine and bake it for 30–40 minutes till it becomes golden
(*3–4 people*)

3. BEAN ROLL ROAST

1 tin half mashed beans in tomato sauce
$\frac{1}{2}$ cup hot water
1 cup grated cheese
Breadcrumbs
2 tablespoons margarine
1 beaten egg
1 chopped onion
Seasoning

Combine the beans, cheese, onion, egg, seasoning and enough crumbs to be able to shape the mixture into a firm roll. Place it on a greased oven dish and pour around it the combined margarine

and hot water. Bake ½ hour or more in a moderate oven, basting it at times with the liquid in the dish. Serve with gravy.
(*3–4 people*)

4. CASHEW NUT ROAST

2 thick trimmed slices brown bread
½ cup chopped cashews
¼ cup other chopped nuts
¼ cup warm oil
113 grams sliced mushrooms
113 grams chopped onions
½ dessertspoon chopped parsley
2 beaten eggs
1 tablespoon margarine
A little stock or milk
Paprika
Salt

Break the bread into bits and soak it for 5 minutes in the stock. Then squeeze out the moisture. In a pan fry the onions and mushrooms. Remove them from the pan and add the bread, ½ the nuts, the egg, parsley and seasoning. Shape the mixture into a loaf and place it in the pan where the onions and mushrooms were fried. Pour the oil over and bake the roast for about 40 minutes, basting it at times with the oil.

5. CHEESE ROLL ROAST

1½ cups flour
1 cup soft or grated cheese
¼ cup margarine
2 tablespoons melted margarine
1½ tablespoons mayonnaise
3 chopped dills
1½ to 2 teaspoons baking powder
2 eggs
Seasoning

Sift the flour, baking powder, seasoning and grate in the $\frac{1}{4}$ cup margarine. With your hands work it into a crumby mixture and add enough mayonnaise for a stiff dough. Chill it and then roll it out into a neat oblong. Spread it with melted margarine and cover the surface with a mixture of soft cheese, a little mayonnaise, the chopped dill, beaten yolks and stiff eggwhites folded in. Roll up the oblong and place it on a greased oven sheet. Bake 30–40 minutes in a 400°F. oven. Serve with sauce or gravy.

(3–4 people)

6. POTATO AND NUT ROAST

$\frac{3}{4}$ cup chopped onions
2 cups mashed potato
$\frac{1}{2}$ cup toasted crumbs
1 cup chopped nuts
2 beaten eggs
$1\frac{1}{2}$ tablespoons melted margarine
$1\frac{1}{2}$ teaspoons mixed herbs
1 teaspoon marmite
Seasoning

Combine the potato, onion, nuts, herbs, marmite, eggs, seasoning. On a floured board shape the mixture into a joint. Place it on a greased oven pan, pour the melted margarine over and roast it for $\frac{1}{2}$ hour. A few nuts may be pushed into the surface of the roast if wished.

(3–4 people)

FRITTERS, CROQUETTES, CUTLETS, RISSOLES, SAUSAGES, STEAKS

1. BEAN CROQUETTES

1 cup cooked mashed beans
½ cup breadcrumbs
¼ cup chopped onion
1 tablespoon flour
2 beaten eggs
1 dessertspoon chopped parsley
½ teaspoon grated lemon rind
Margarine or oil
Seasoning

Combine the beans, ½ the breadcrumbs, flour, 1 beaten egg, seasoning. Fry the onion and add it. The mixture should be firm. With floured hands shape round or flat cakes. Dip them into beaten egg and then into crumbs. Fry the cakes golden. N.B. Peas or lentils may be used instead of beans.

2. BEAN SOUP FRITTERS

1 tin bean soup
¼–½ cup flour
¼ cup chopped onion
1 beaten egg
3 tablespoons stale breadcrumbs
1½ teaspoons baking powder
Garlic salt
Oil
Seasoning

Combine all the ingredients but the oil for a firm mixture. Drop spoonfuls in deep hot oil and cook golden. Drain.

3. Bean Cutlets

227 grams soaked, cooked, sieved dry beans
1 large skinned sliced tomato
1 cup stock or water
2 tablespoons flour
2 tablespoons margarine
1 beaten egg
100 grams breadcrumbs
75 grams seedless raisins
1 teaspoon curry powder
Seasoning

Fry the tomato 5 minutes and add the combined flour, curry powder, seasoning, mixing. Gradually add the stock, stirring. Then add the sieved beans, raisins, $\frac{1}{2}$ the breadcrumbs and cook 3 minutes. Remove pan from the heat and chill. On a floured board divide the mixture into portions and shape them into cutlets. Dip them into the egg and the crumbs and fry or bake golden.
(3–4 people)

4. Bean Sausages

1 cup cooked mashed beans
$\frac{1}{2}$ cup crumbs or mashed potato
Extra crumbs
$\frac{1}{4}$ cup chopped peanuts
1 small chopped onion
1 beaten egg
1 tablespoon chopped parsley or mixed herbs
Margarine
Seasoning

Combine all but the egg and with floured hands shape the mixture into sausages. Dip them into the egg and then into crumbs. Fry them golden.

5. BEETROOT FRITTERS

1 cup cooked mashed beetroots
1 cup breadcrumbs and extra crumbs
¾ cup milk
2 beaten eggs
Melted margarine
Paprika
Salt

Soak the cup of crumbs in milk and squeeze them partly dry. Add the beetroot, eggs, seasoning. With floured hands shape flat cakes. Dip them in the extra crumbs and fry them golden.
(*3–4 people*)

6. BREAD STEAKS

6 trimmed and cubed bread slices
85 grams breadcrumbs
1 beaten egg
Milk
3 teaspoons chopped parsley
¼ teaspoon mixed herbs
Margarine
Seasoning

Combine the cubed bread, parsley, herbs, seasoning. Moisten this with milk for a firm mixture. Mash it and with floured hands shape steaks. Cover them with crumbs and dip them into the beaten egg. Again cover them with crumbs and fry golden.
(*3–4 people*)

7. CARROT SAUSAGES

2 cups grated carrots
½ cup chopped onion
2 tablespoons flour
1 tablespoon chopped parsley
Breadcrumbs
3 eggs
½ teaspoon nutmeg
Oil or melted margarine
A little milk
Seasoning

Combine the carrot, onion, flour, parsley, nutmeg, 1 tablespoon melted margarine, seasoning and enough milk for a firm mixture. With floured hands shape sausages. Dip them in beaten egg and then into breadcrumbs. Fry them golden.
(*3–4 people*)

8. CAULIFLOWER FRITTERS

1½ cups cooked cauliflower florets
2 tablespoons flour
1 chopped onion
2 large beaten eggs
½ teaspoon thyme
Oil
Cayenne
Salt

Mash the cauliflower roughly and add the onion, flour, eggs, thyme, seasoning. With floured hands shape fritters and fry them golden *or* drop spoonfuls into deep hot fat and cook golden.

9. CHEESE CREAM FRITTERS

1½ cups batter
¾ cup cheese cream
Margarine
2 teaspoons chopped onion
2 teaspoons chopped parsley
1 teaspoon mixed herbs
Seasoning

Batter:
1 cup milk
¼ cup flour
1 large beaten egg
Salt

Combine the flour, egg, milk, and beat smooth. Add the onion, parsley, herbs, seasoning and with the mixture fry small fritters. Spread the surface of each one with cheese cream and roll them up and place them in a serving dish.

Cheese Cream:
4 tablespoons grated cheese
2 tablespoons top milk
1 teaspoon made mustard.

In a double boiler combine the ingredients and stir till smooth. Do not boil.
  These are nice with bean dishes.

10. CHEESE CUTLETS

1 cup grated cheddar
½ cup enriched mashed potato
½ cup breadcrumbs
1 to 2 beaten eggs
Margarine
Paprika
Seasoning

Combine all but the margarine. If too dry add a little milk for a firm mixture. With floured hands shape cutlets and fry them golden. Serve with scrambled eggs or fried tomato.

11. CHEESE ROUNDS

1 large cup grated cheese
1 large cup breadcrumbs
½ cup chopped walnuts
½ to ¾ cup parsley water
1 beaten egg
½ teaspoon lemon juice
Seasoning

Combine the dry ingredients and add the lemon juice and enough parsley water for a not too stiff mixture. Drop spoonfuls on a greased oven sheet and bake golden *or* drop spoonfuls into deep hot fat and cook golden.
(*3–4 people*)

12. FRITTERS WITH MUSHROOMS

227 grams soft breadcrumbs
85 grams melted margarine
Extra margarine
½ cup milk
2 beaten eggs
1 tablespoon chopped onions or leeks
1 dessertspoon chopped parsley
1 teaspoon mixed herbs
Seasoning
1 cup sliced mushrooms
Brown gravy
Red currant jelly

Mix the breadcrumbs and melted margarine. Add the onion, parsley, herbs, seasoning. Then add the eggs and enough milk for a

firm mixture. Shape portions into fritters or fingers and fry them golden. Serve with fried mushrooms, gravy and the jelly.
(*3–4 people*)

13. Hard Egg Rissoles

1 cup cracker crumbs
1 cup white sauce
4 chopped hard eggs
1 beaten raw egg
Margarine or oil
2 tablespoons chopped onion
1 tablespoon chopped parsley or green pepper
¼ cup cold water
¼ teaspoon nutmeg
Seasoning

Combine the hard eggs, onion, parsley, nutmeg, seasoning and enough white sauce for a firm mixture. With floured hands shape rissoles. Dip them into the combined raw egg and water and then into the cracker crumbs. Fry golden in hot fat and drain them.

14. Macaroni Fritters

85 grams cooked chopped macaroni
170 grams breadcrumbs moistened with a little water
4 boiled chopped onions
2 beaten eggs
Margarine
¼ teaspoon paprika
Seasoning
Brown gravy

Combine the fine chopped macaroni, the onion, moist breadcrumbs, paprika, seasoning. With floured hands shape fritters. Fry them golden. Serve with the gravy.
(*3–4 people*)

15. Nut and Olive Croquettes

1½ cups soft breadcrumbs
½ cup chopped olives
½ cup chopped walnuts
1 tablespoon chopped onion
2 beaten eggs
Oil or margarine
Seasoning
A little milk if necessary

Combine all the ingredients but the oil for a firm mixture. Shape portions into small croquettes, using some of the crumbs if they are too soft. Roll them in crumbs and fry them golden.

16. Oatmeal Fritters

1½ cups oatmeal porridge
1 cup grated cheese
1 teaspoon made mustard
2 tablespoons flour
1 tablespoon margarine
1 beaten egg
Cayenne,
Salt

Combine all ingredients but the margarine. Drop spoonfuls into deep hot fat and cook golden. Drain them.
(*3–4 people*)

17. POACHED EGG FRITTERS

4 poached eggs
1 cup batter
¼ cup wine vinegar
Fried onion or parsley
57 grams margarine
1 teaspoon mixed herbs
Seasoning

Cool the poached eggs in cold water. Remove them from it and pour over them the combined vinegar and herbs. Let them soak in this for 15 to 20 minutes. Then drain and dry them and dip them thoroughly in the batter which should be rather firm. Fry them golden and serve with the fried onion or parsley.

The Batter:
1 cup flour
½ cup stock
½ cup water
1½ teaspoons baking powder
Salt

18. PEANUT BUTTER SAUSAGES

1 cup mashed potato
1 beaten egg
1 level dessertspoon peanut butter
Fried onion rings
2 teaspoons chopped parsley
½ teaspoon mixed herbs
A little milk
Margarine
seasoning

Combine the potato, peanut butter, parsley, herbs seasoning and enough milk for a firm mixture. With floured hands shape sausages. Place them on a greased oven dish and bake them golden.

Paint them with melted margarine and bake a minute more. Serve with the fried onion rings.

19. POTATO AND CHEESE FRITTERS

2 cups mashed potato
1 cup grated Cheddar
2 beaten eggs
2 to 3 tablespoons flour
A little milk
1 tablespoon chopped parsley or green pepper
1 teaspoon made mustard
1½ teaspoons baking powder
Oil
Cayenne
Salt

Combine the potato, flour, cheese, mustard, parsley, seasoning, eggs and add enough milk for a firm mixture. Drop spoonfuls into hot oil and cook golden *or* shape the mixture into fritters and fry them golden.
(*3–4 people*)

20. RICE RISSOLES

2 cups cooked rice
½ cup brown breadcrumbs
2 chopped hard eggs
2 skinned sieved tomatoes
1 small chopped onion
2 teaspoon chopped parsley
Seasoning
Oil

Combine all but the oil. With floured hands shape the mixture into rissoles. Heat the oil and fry them golden. Drain them.
(*4–5 people*)

21. Soya Bean Croquettes

1 cup cooked mashed Soya or other beans
1 cup chopped nuts
½ cup cooked rice
2 beaten eggs
1 small chopped onion
Breadcrumbs
Oil
Seasoning
Pineapple rings

Combine, beans, nuts, onion, rice, 1 egg, seasoning and with floured hands shape croquettes. Dip them in beaten egg and then into the crumbs. Place them on a greased oven sheet and bake them golden *or* fry them golden in oil. Grill the pineapple rings golden and serve them with the croquettes.
(*3–4 people*)

22. Spinach Fritters

1 cup cooked chopped spinach
1 cup grated cheese
3 beaten eggs
1½ to 2 tablespoons flour
Breadcrumbs
Margarine
Cayenne
Garlic salt

Combine the spinach, cheese, flour, cayenne, garlic salt and 2 beaten eggs. With floured hands shape portions of the mixture into fritters. Dip them in egg and then into the crumbs. Fry them golden.

23. Sweetcorn Fritters

1 cup sweetcorn kernels
¼ cup chopped olives or dills
¼ cup flour
2 eggs
A little milk
2 teaspoons baking powder
Oil
Seasoning

Sieve the flour, baking powder, seasoning into a bowl and in the centre make a hollow. Into it break the eggs and corn. Add enough milk for a firm mixture. Drop spoonfuls of it into deep hot oil *or* fry golden the fritters you have shaped.

24. Tinned Bean Croquettes

1½ cups tinned drained beans
¼ cup flour
¼ cup cracker crumbs
2 beaten eggs
Oil
1 small chopped onion
1 tablespoon chopped parsley
1½ teaspoons baking powder
Margarine or oil
Seasoning

Combine all the ingredients but one beaten egg and the oil. With floured hands shape portions of the mixture into croquettes. Dip them into the other beaten egg diluted with a little water, and then into the cracker crumbs. Fry golden and then drain them. Cooked peas or lentils may be used instead of the beans.
(*3–4 people*)

MEAL BAKES

1. ASPARAGUS BAKE

1 tin drained asparagus tips
1 tin asparagus soup
3 tablespoons grated cheese
3 quartered hard eggs
1 beaten raw egg
Margarine
Seasoning

In a greased oven dish place the asparagus. On it arrange the hard egg pieces. Pour over the combined soup, beaten raw egg, seasoning. Sprinkle with the cheese and dot with margarine. Bake till set in a 325–350°F. oven.
(*3–4 people*)

2. ASPARAGUS AND SWEETCORN BAKE

1 tin asparagus cuts
1 tin sweetcorn
2 chopped hard eggs
1 cup milk
Topping
2 tablespoons flour
1 tablespoon chopped parsley or green pepper
Margarine
Seasoning
Cayenne

Heat the asparagus liquid and to it add a paste of flour and milk, and stir till thickened and smooth. Now add the asparagus, sweetcorn, egg, parsley, cayenne, seasoning. Place the mixture in a greased oven dish and cover it with the topping. Dot with margarine and bake about ½ hour in a moderate oven.

Topping:
$\frac{3}{4}$ cup breadcrumbs
$\frac{1}{2}$ cup coconut
113 grams grated cheese
Combine the ingredients.
(*3–4 people*)

3. BEAN AND TOMATO BAKE

1 Beaten egg
$1\frac{1}{2}$ cups cooked drained beans
$1\frac{1}{4}$ cups skinned chopped tomato
1 large chopped carrot
1 chopped onion
Margarine
$\frac{1}{2}$ teaspoon thyme
Seasoning

Fry the onion soft. Add the tomato and carrot. Cook a little, stirring. Remove the pan from the fire and add the rest of the ingredients. Place the mixture in a greased oven dish and bake about $\frac{1}{2}$ hour in a moderate oven.

4. BEAN AND OATMEAL BAKE

1 tin baked beans with tomato sauce
$\frac{1}{2}$ cup grated cheese
2 tablespoons cooked oatmeal
1 beaten egg
Margarine
Breadcrumbs
Seasoning

Half mash the beans and add $\frac{1}{2}$ the cheese, the oatmeal, the egg and seasoning. Place the mixture in a greased oven dish. Sprinkle it with the combined breadcrumbs and rest of the cheese. Dot with margarine and bake 15 to 20 minutes in a 400°F. oven.

5. Brinjal Bake

1 boiled brinjal
$\frac{3}{4}$ cup grated cheese
2 beaten eggs
$1\frac{1}{2}$ tablespoons flour
1 tablespoon melted margarine
2 tablespoons milk
Seasoning

Peel the brinjal and remove the seeds. Mash it and add the flour, cheese, margarine, seasoning. Place the mixture in a flat greased oven dish and pour over the combined eggs and milk. Bake till set in a 325°F. oven.

6. Broadbean Bake

454 grams young and tender broadbeans
2 cups milk
3 beaten eggs
$\frac{1}{4}$ teaspoon nutmeg
1 tablespoon chopped onion
$\frac{1}{2}$ tablespoon chopped parsley
Seasoning

Slice the broadbeans (pods and all) across as you would for green beans. In a pan just cover them with water and cook them for about 20 minutes. Drain and place them in an oven dish. Pour over them the combined eggs, milk, onion, parsley, seasoning. Sprinkle with nutmeg and place the dish in a pan of water. Bake it for about 40 minutes till set in a 325°F. oven.

7. Carrot and Pea Bake

227 grams diced fresh carrots
227 grams fresh peas
½ cup grated cheese
1 small chopped onion
½ cup vegetable water
1½ tablespoons breadcrumbs
1½ tablespoons flour
1½ tablespoons margarine
½ tablespoon chopped parsley
½ teaspoon dry mustard
Seasoning

Cook the carrots and peas tender. Drain them and keep the vegetable water. Place them in a greased oven dish. Fry the onion soft and sprinkle it with the flour, mixing. Gradually add 1 cup of the vegetable water and stir till the mixture thickens. Add the seasoning and remove the pan from the fire. Add the combined cheese and mustard and stir till the cheese melts. Add the parsley and pour the sauce over the vegetables. Sprinkle with crumbs, dot with margarine and bake golden.
(*3–4 people*)

8. Carrot and Sweetcorn Bake

1 tin sweetcorn
1 cup shredded carrots
1 cup hot milk
¼ cup chopped green pepper *or* parsley
2 beaten eggs
2 tablespoons chopped onion
2 tablespoons flour
2 tablespoons margarine
½ teaspoon paprika
Seasoning

In a double boiler make a white sauce with the margarine, flour and milk. Add the paprika and seasoning. Let cool a little and add the eggs. Add the carrot and onion and place the mixture in a greased oven dish. Bake about 40 minutes in a moderate oven. (*3–4 people*)

9. Cauliflower and Custard Bake

1 cup cooked cauliflower sprigs
1¾ cups milk
2 beaten eggs
½ chopped onion
3 teaspoons chopped parsley
Margarine
Cayenne
Salt

Fry the onion just golden and add the cauliflower pieces and parsley. Cook 5 minutes and place the mixture in a greased oven dish. Pour over the combined eggs, milk, cayenne, seasoning. Bake about 40 minutes in a 325°F. oven.

10. Cheese and Tomato Bake

3 skinned sliced tomatoes
2 boiled sliced onions
1 cup brown breadcrumbs
¾ cup grated cheese
3 sliced hard eggs
1½ teaspoons sugar
Seasoning
Sauce
Margarine

In a greased oven dish place the tomato slices and sprinkle them with sugar and seasoning. Cover them with the onion and sprinkle with ½ the cheese. Over this arrange the egg slices. Then pour the sauce over and sprinkle with the combined crumbs and rest of the cheese. Dot with margarine and bake 20 minutes in a 400°F. oven.

Sauce:
1 tablespoon flour
1 tablespoon margarine
3 tablespoons grated cheese
½ cup milk
½ teaspoon made mustard

Melt the margarine and add the flour, blending. Gradually add the milk and stir till smooth. Add the cheese and stir till melted. Then add the mustard and seasoning.

11. CHEESE AND NUT BAKE

1½ cups warm mashed potato
½ cup grated Cheddar
½ cup chopped nuts
¾ cup milk
2 beaten eggs
1 tablespoon margarine
¾ teaspoon nutmeg
Seasoning

To plain mashed potatoes add the margarine, ½ the cheese and nuts, the milk and the seasoning. Add the eggs and place the mixture in a greased oven dish. To the rest of the cheese and nuts add the nutmeg and prinkle it over the mixture. Bake golden in a 400°F. oven.

12. Cheese Bananas

5 Bananas halved lengthwise
1 cup grated cheddar
1 cup breadcrumbs
¾ cup top *or* Ideal milk
2 tablespoons melted margarine
Seasoning

Place the bananas in a greased oven dish and cover them with the combined cheese, crumbs, margarine, Ideal milk, seasoning. Bake 30 to 40 minutes in a 400°F. oven.

13. Corn and Mushroom Bake

1 small packet kernel corn
113 grams sliced mushrooms
¼ cup buttermilk or yoghurt
¼ cup rice
2 tablespoon chopped onion
1 tablespoon peeled chopped cucumber *or* chopped green pepper
1½ tablespoons margarine
2 teaspoon soya sauce
½ teaspoon mixed herbs
1 cup milk with 1 beaten egg

Fry the onion 5 minutes and add the mushrooms, cucumber, soya sauce and cook another 5 minutes. Remove the pan from the fire and add the rice, corn, buttermilk, seasoning. Place the mixture in a greased oven dish. Sprinkle it with the herbs and cover the dish. Bake 30 to 40 minutes in a moderate oven. Uncover the dish for the last 5 or 6 minutes of baking.

14. DRIED PEA BAKE

454 grams soaked dried peas cooked with a pinch of soda
1 large chopped onion
½ cup grated cheese
½ cup breadcrumbs
½ cup vegetable stock
1 cup white sauce
2 tablespoons margarine
Seasoning

Fry the onion soft with 1 tablespoon margarine. Remove the onion from the pan and in it place the rest of the margarine in which to fry the breadcrumbs. When they have become golden place a layer of them in a greased oven dish. Cover them with a layer of the peas and then of fried onion. Repeat these layers, using seasoning, and end with a layer of peas. Pour the white sauce over and sprinkle with the rest of the fried crumbs combined with the rest of the cheese. Dot with margarine and bake golden in a 400°F. oven. (*3–4 people*)

15. EGG AND ONION BAKE

4 hard egg chunks
3 boiled onion Chunks
2 cups white sauce
1 teaspoon made mustard
¼ cup grated cheddar
¼ cup breadcrumbs
1 tablespoon margarine
Cayenne
Salt

Combine the white sauce, onion, egg chunks, cayenne, mustard, salt. Place the mixture in a greased oven dish. Sprinkle it with combined cheese and crumbs. Dot with margarine and bake golden in a moderate oven.
(*3–4 people*)

16. Egg and Soup Bake

6 thin trimmed slices buttered bread
1¾ cups milk and water
1 packet soup powder
2 to 3 beaten eggs
½ cup grated Cheddar
Seasoning

Quarter the bread slices and with them line a greased oven dish. Simmer the combined soup powder, milk and water for about 10 minutes. Remove the pan from the fire and let the mixture cool for a few minutes. Then add the cheese, eggs and seasoning and pour the mixture into the lined dish. Bake till set in a medium oven. (*3–4 people*)

17. Green Pea Bake

1½ cups soaked, cooked peas
½ cup breadcrumbs
1 tablespoon peanut butter
2 beaten eggs
Vegetable water
2 chopped celery sticks *or* ¼ chopped green pepper
1 grated parsnip *or* turnip
Fresh or dry mint to taste
Seasoning

Cook the celery tender and mash it after it has been drained. Half mash the peas and add them to the celery. Add the rest of the ingredients and enough vegetable water for a slack mixture. Place it in a greased oven dish and bake 30 to 40 minutes in a moderate oven.

18. Lentil Bake

1½ cups soaked, cooked, sieved lentils
¾ cup top or Ideal milk
2 large eggs
Gravy
¾ teaspoon sage
¼ teaspoon thyme
Seasoning

Combine all but the eggs and the gravy. Add the beaten egg yolks and fold in the stiffly beaten whites. Place the mixture in a greased oven dish and bake 20 to 30 minutes. Serve with gravy.

19. Mushroom and Tomato Bake

1 tin chopped mushrooms
1½ cups enriched mashed potato
1 cup fresh breadcrumbs
1 cup grated cheese
1 to 2 skinned sliced tomatoes
1 chopped onion
Margarine or oil
2 teaspoons chopped parsley
1 teaspoon sugar
Seasoning

Fry the onion soft and add the mushrooms and their liquid. Remove the pan from the fire and add the breadcrumbs, stirring. Place the mixture in a greased oven dish. On it arrange the tomato slices. Sprinkle them with the sugar and seasoning. Cover them with the mashed potato and sprinkle it with the cheese. Bake golden in a 400°F oven..

Enriched mashed potato: To the mashed potato add a little warm milk, some margarine and a little seasoning.
(3–4 people)

20. Onion and Egg Bake

4–5 sliced onions
$\frac{3}{4}$ cup cooked green peas
$\frac{1}{4}$ cup chopped celery or parsley
$\frac{1}{2}$ cup breadcrumbs
4 hard quartered eggs
2 cups milk
$1\frac{1}{2}$ tablespoons margarine
$1\frac{1}{2}$ tablespoons flour
3 tablespoons grated cheese
Paprika
Salt

Boil the onions tender and drain them. Place a layer of them in a greased oven dish. On this arrange $\frac{1}{2}$ the egg pieces and on them place half the combined peas and celery. Cover with a white sauce made with margarine, flour, milk, cheese and seasoning. Sprinkle with crumbs and paprika. Dot with margarine. Bake till golden. (*3–4 people*)

21. Potato and Nut Bake

$1\frac{1}{2}$ cups mashed potato
$\frac{3}{4}$ cup grated cheese
$\frac{1}{2}$ cup warm milk
2 beaten eggs
2 tablespoons melted margarine
57 grams chopped pecans *or* walnuts
$\frac{1}{4}$ teaspoon nutmeg
Seasoning

Combine the potato, half the margarine, the milk, $\frac{3}{4}$ of the cheese and nuts and the seasoning. Add the eggs and place the mixture in a greased oven dish. Sprinkle with the rest of the cheese, nuts and margarine.

22. POTATO AND MUSHROOM BAKE

1½ cups peeled, cooked, sliced potatoes
½ cup sliced mushrooms
1 medium sliced onion
1 *thick* trimmed bread slice
½ cup chopped nuts
2 hard chopped eggs
2–3 tablespoons schmaltz
1½ tablespoons salad oil
¼ teaspoon nutmeg
¼ teaspoon Basil
Breadcrumbs
Seasoning

Fry the onion and mushrooms 5 minutes in the oil and remove them from the pan. To them add the bread soaked in water and squeezed dry, the nuts, eggs, nutmeg, Basil, seasoning, and toss the mixture with 1 tablespoon of schmaltz. In an oven dish greased with schmaltz place a layer of the sliced potatoes and cover it with a layer of the onion mixture. Continue the layers, ending with a layer of the potato. Sprinkle with combined schmaltz and breadcrumbs. Bake 30–40 minutes in a 375°F. oven.
(*3–4 people*)

23. POTATO AND OLIVE BAKE

1½ cups peeled, cooked sliced potatoes
4 lightly fried eggs
½ cup top *or* Ideal milk
10 chopped black olives
4 tablespoons grated cheese
2 tablespoons melted margarine
Brown breadcrumbs
Seasoning

Sprinkle a greased oven dish with a thin layer of the breadcrumbs. On them place the potatoes and on them the olives. Over them place the fried eggs and sprinkle them with seasoning. Cover with a layer of crumbs and pour the milk over. Now pour over the melted margarine and bake about $\frac{1}{2}$ hour in a 400°F. oven.

24. Pineapple and Bean Bake

$1\frac{1}{2}$ cups soaked cooked, drained beans
1 small tin pineapple chunks drained
$\frac{1}{2}$ cup halved button mushrooms
2 slices trimmed bread squares
1 small sliced onion
$\frac{3}{4}$ cup mashed potatoes
2 beaten eggs
3 tablespoons oil
1 tablespoons soya sauce
Seasoning

Fry the onion and mushrooms 5 minutes in the oil and add the bread cubes, tossing till they have absorbed the oil. Add all the rest of the ingredients but the mashed potatoes. Place the mixture in a greased oven dish and bake 30 minutes in a moderate oven. Cover with mashed potatoes and bake till golden.
(*3–4 people*)

25. Spinach and Soup Bake

$1\frac{1}{2}$ cups partly cooked spinach
$\frac{3}{4}$ cups mushroom soup
6–7 thin slices Cheddar
5 sliced hard eggs
3 teaspoons melted margarine
$\frac{1}{4}$ teaspoon nutmeg
Seasoning

In a greased oven dish place the egg slices spread out. Over them arrange the cheese slices and on top of them place a layer of combined spinach, melted margarine and seasoning. Cover with the soup and sprinkle with nutmeg. Bake about 15 minutes in a moderate oven.

26. STUFFED EGG BAKE

2 cups mashed potato enriched with margarine, warm milk and
   egg and seasoning
5 hard eggs halved lengthwise
1 small chopped onion
1 tablespoon chopped parsley
1 tablespoon margarine
3 teaspoons tomato sauce
Breadcrumbs
Seasoning

Combine the mashed egg yolks, onion, parsley, tomato sauce, seasoning and stuff the hollow egg whites with the mixture. On a greased oven dish place a thick layer of the mashed potato. On it press in at equal distances the stuffed eggwhites. Sprinkle with crumbs and dot with margarine. Bake golden.
(*3–4 people*)

27. TOMATO PUREE AND BEANS

2–3 skinned sliced tomatoes
2 cups soaked, cooked beans
$\frac{3}{4}$ cup grated cheddar
1 chopped onion
1 tablespoon margarine
$\frac{1}{2}$ tablespoon brown sugar
1 teaspoon made mustard
Seasoning

Cook the tomato and onion till tender and half reduced. Sieve this and place it in a saucepan. Add all but the beans and the cheese and stir till smooth. Then add the cheese and stir till melted. Pour the puree over the warm beans.

28. TOMATO AND GREEN PEA BAKE

1 tin green peas
2 beaten eggs
1½ cups milk
1 tablespoon margarine
1 large skinned chopped tomato
1 medium chopped onion
3 teaspoons chopped parsley
Seasoning to taste
½ teaspoon sugar

Fry the onion 5 minutes and remove the pan from the fire. To it add the peas, tomato, sugar, parsley, seasoning and place the mixture in an oven dish. Over it pour the combined eggs, milk, seasoning and place the dish in a pan of water. Bake till set in a moderate oven.

CURRY DISHES

1. BABOTIE

$\frac{3}{4}$ cup chopped nuts
$\frac{3}{4}$ cup chopped onion
$\frac{3}{4}$ cup chopped carrot
$\frac{3}{4}$ cup soft breadcrumbs
$\frac{1}{2}$ cup hot water
Custard
Orange or bay leaves
2 teaspoons curry powder
2 teaspoons chutney
1 teaspoons lemon juice
1 teaspoon apricot jam
$\frac{1}{2}$ teaspoon tumeric
$\frac{1}{2}$ teaspoon marmite
1 dessertspoon oil
Seasoning

Fry the onion and add the rest of the ingredients *but* the leaves, custard, hot water and marmite. Toss the mixture and gradually add the combined hot water and marmite. Place this in a greased oven dish and bake for 30–40 minutes in a moderate oven. Then pour the custard over and bake it until it sets, after having inserted the leaves.

Custard: 1 cup of milk, 2 small beaten eggs, seasoning

2. Babotie with Raisins

2 cups brown breadcrumbs
1 cup chopped nuts
1 cup hot water
2 chopped onions
2 grated carrots
Custard
Bay leaves
Seasoning
1 tablespoon curry powder
2 tablespoons seedless raisins
1 tablespoon coconut
½ tablespoon chutney
½ tablespoon vinegar
1 tablespoon margarine
2 teaspoons apricot jam
1 teaspoon tumeric
1 teaspoon marmite

Fry the onions and remove the pan from the fire. Add the rest of the ingredients *but* the custard and bayleaves. Place the mixture in a greased oven dish and pour the custard over. Insert a few bayleaves and bake till the custard sets in a 325°F. oven.

Custard: 1 cup milk, 1 large beaten egg, seasoning

3. Curried Beans

2 cups soaked cooked beans
1½ cups stock or water
1½ grated carrot
1 small chopped apple
1 small chopped onion
1 tablespoon flour
1 tablespoon oil or margarine
2–3 teaspoons curry powder
Seasoning
Warm cooked rice

Fry onion, carrot, apple tender. Add combined flour, curry powder, seasoning and mix. Gradually add the stock, stirring till thickened. Add the beans and heat well. Serve this with the rice. N.B. Peas, soya beans or lentils may be used instead of beans. (*3–4 people*)

4. CURRIED BEAN BAKE

2 cups soaked cooked beans
1½ cups stock or water
2 small skinned chopped tomatoes
2 beaten eggs
¼ cup seedless raisins
½ cup breadcrumbs
1½ tablespoon margarine
1 tablespoons flour
½ tablespoon curry powder
Seasoning

Mash and sieve the beans. Fry the tomato tender and add the combined flour, curry powder and seasoning. Gradually add the stock, stirring till smooth. Remove from the fire and add the bean mash and rest of ingredients. Place the mixture in a greased oven dish and bake 30 minutes in a moderate oven.

5. CURRIED CARROT BAKE

1½ cups shredded carrots
1 cup cooked rice
1 cup grated cheese
1 cup milk
2 beaten eggs
2 tablespoons chopped onion
2 teaspoons curry powder
Seasoning

Combine all ingredients but some of the cheese, and place the mixture in a greased oven dish. Sprinkle with the rest of the cheese. Bake 30–40 minutes in a moderate oven.

6. CURRIED EGGS

Cooked rice
4–5 halved hard eggs
1 sliced onion
$\frac{1}{4}$ cup sliced olives
Stock or water
1 tablespoon margarine
1 tablespoon flour
$\frac{1}{4}$ tablespoon curry powder
$\frac{1}{4}$ tablespoon vinegar
1 tablespoon vinegar
1 teaspoons sugar
Seasoning

Fry the onion tender and add the combined flour, curry powder, sugar, vinegar, seasoning. Mix well and gradually add enough water for a medium thick sauce. Add the olives. Place the egg halves on the rice and serve with the sauce.

7. CURRIED EGG STEW

6 hard eggs
$1\frac{1}{2}$ cups skinned quartered tomatoes
$\frac{1}{2}$ cup warm water
Seasoning
2 small sliced onions
$1\frac{1}{2}$ tablespoons margarine
1 dessertspoon curry powder

Prick the eggs all over with a knitting needle and roll them all over in combined curry powder and seasoning. Fry the onions soft and add the leftover curry powder. Add the tomatoes and warm water and cook, stirring, till well thickened. Add the eggs and simmer gently for 5 minutes. Serve with rice or macaroni.

8. MEALIE RICE CURRY

2 cups cooked mealie rice
1 cup milk
1½ tablespoons margarine
2 beaten eggs
1 large skinned sliced tomato
1 large sliced onion
2 teaspoons curry powder
½ teaspoon mixed herbs
Seasoning

Fry the onion soft and remove the pan from the fire. Add the rest of the ingredients. Toss them and then place the mixture in a greased oven dish. Bake 20–30 minutes till golden.

9. SPAGHETTI CURRY

2 cups cooked spaghetti pieces
2 cups grated cheese
1½ cups stock
¼ cup tomato ketchup
2 chopped hard eggs
Bayleaf
1½ tablespoons flour
1½ tablespoons melted margarine
2 teaspoons curry powder
3 teaspoons chopped parsley
1 teaspoon oil
¼ teaspoon thyme
salt

Cook the spaghetti in water to which the oil has been added. Drain and keep it warm. In a double boiler blend the margarine and flour. Gradually add the combined stock and tomato puree, stirring till thickened. Add a paste made with the curry powder and a little water. Add the cheese and stir till it melts. Remove the top pan from the heat and add the eggs and parsley. Pour the sauce over the spaghetti and toss it. Serve with potato chips.

10. SPANISH CURRIED BEANS

1 cup cooked, half mashed beans
½ cup grated cheese
¾ cup skinned chopped tomatoes
¾ cup breadcrumbs
½ cup chopped onion
2 beaten eggs
Enough stock to moisten well
1½ tablespoons margarine
2 teaspoons curry powder
2 teaspoons chutney
1 teaspoon made mustard
3 teaspoons chopped parsley
½ teaspoon thyme
Seasoning

Fry onion soft and add the curry powder, mixing. Add the beans, stock, tomato, chutney, mustard, mixing and the parsley, half the cheese, thyme, eggs, seasoning and simmer a few minutes. Remove the pan from the fire and place the mixture in a greased oven dish. Sprinkle it with the rest of the cheese mixed with crumbs. Dot with margarine and bake golden.

11. Stewed Banana and Nut Curry

5 peeled bananas cut into chunks
1 peeled chopped apple
1 large chopped onion
1 cup milk with 1 cup water
$\frac{1}{4}$ cup sultanas
2 tablespoons flour
2 tablespoons margarine
1 dessertspoon curry powder
1 dessertspoon chutney
Seasoning

Fry onion soft, not brown. Add the apple, bananas, sultanas, seasoning and cook 5 minutes. Mix in the combined flour and curry powder and gradually add the combined milk and water. Cook and stir till thickened. Add the chutney and heat. Serve with rice.

12. Sweetcorn Curry

$1\frac{1}{2}$ cups cooked rice
1 cup sweetcorn
3 whole hard eggs
2 halved hard eggs
Curry mayonnaise
Seasoning
1 stick chopped celery or celery leaves
$\frac{1}{2}$ chopped green pepper
3 sliced bananas
1–1$\frac{1}{2}$ tablespoons oil
1 tablespoon vinegar
1 teaspoon sugar

Combine the rice, green pepper, celery, drained corn, combined oil, vinegar and sugar and toss the mixture thoroughly. Make a heap of it on a serving dish and on it arrange the whole and halved eggs. Serve with the curry mayonnaise.

Curry mayonnaise:
½ cup mayonnaise
2 tablespoons top milk
2 tablespoon red wine
½ tablespoon oil
1 tablespoon smooth apricot jam
1 small chopped onion
1½–2 teaspoons curry powder
1½–2 teaspoons tomato chutney
1 teaspoon lemon juice
1 teaspoon sugar
Paprika
Salt

Fry the onion soft. Add the curry powder and cook 1 minute. Add the combined tomato chutney, wine, lemon juice, sugar, jam, paprika, salt. Cook a few minutes and remove the pan from the fire. Let the mixture cool a little and then add the combined mayonnaise and top milk.

13. TINNED SWEETCORN CURRY

1 tin sweetcorn
2 cups cooked rice
1½ cups stock
5–6 sliced hard eggs
1 chopped onion
1 chopped apple
1½ tablespoons flour
2 tablespoons margarine
½ dessertspoon curry powder
1½ teaspoons lemon juice
1 teaspoon sugar
2 teaspoons chutney
Seasoning

Fry onion golden and add and stir in the combined flour and curry powder. Gradually add the combined stock, lemon juice, sugar, chutney, seasoning and stir till the mixture thickens. Add the apple and simmer 10–15 minutes. Place the warm combined rice and sweetcorn on a serving dish and pour the sauce over. Decorate with hard egg slices.

(*3–4 people*)

NON MEAT STEWS

1. Avocado and Mushroom Stew

1 peeled avocado in chunks
1 cup sliced mushrooms
1 cup milk
$\frac{1}{4}$ cup top milk *or* Ideal milk
$1\frac{1}{2}$ tablespoons flour
2 tablespoons margarine
1 desertspoon brandy
Paprika
Salt

In half the margarine fry the mushrooms 5 minutes. Remove them from the pan and in it place the rest of the margarine and stir till melted. Add the flour and blend it in. Gradually add the combined milks and stir till thickened. Return the mushrooms to the pan and add the brandy and seasoning. Simmer 5 minutes and add the avocado chunks. Cook till heated but not boiling. Place the mixture in a serving dish and sprinkle with paprika. Serve with rice.

2. Bean and Rice Stew

1 tin baked beans
2 cups cooked rice
$1\frac{1}{2}$ cups white sauce
3–4 sliced hard eggs
$1\frac{1}{2}$ tablespoons margarine
1 tablespoon chopped parsley
1 chopped onion
$\frac{1}{2}$ teaspoon garlic salt
$\frac{1}{4}$ teaspoon ground cloves
$\frac{1}{4}$ teaspoon red pepper

Fry the onion and add the parsley, garlic salt, red pepper. Combine this with the rice and beans. Add the white sauce and place the mixture on a serving dish. Decorate with the egg slices.

3. BEAN AND WALNUT STEW

1 tin haricot beans
½ cup chopped walnuts
½ cup chopped boiled onions
½ cup Ideal milk
1 tablespoon chopped parsley
¼ teaspoon nutmeg
¼ teaspoon red pepper
¼ teaspoon salt

Combine the beans, onion, seasoning and cook gently for 6–7 minutes. Add the walnuts and simmer a few minutes. Place the mixture in a serving dish and sprinkle it with parsley.
(*3–4 people*)

4. BUTTER BEAN STEW

2 cups soaked cooked butter beans
¾ cup grated carrots
1½ cups stock
3 diced hard eggs
1 chopped onion
1½ tablespoons flour
1½ tablespoons margarine
Seasoning

Cook onion and carrots tender and drain them. With the margarine, flour, stock and seasoning make a white sauce. Add the cooked onion and carrot, the beans and egg pieces. Heat without boiling and serve.

5. CORN AND SPINACH STEW

1 cup sweetcorn
1½ cup cooked chopped spinach
¾ cup peeled, seeded, chopped tomato
1 chopped onion
7–8 stoned, chopped black olives
1 tablespoon wine vinegar
5–6 tablespoons water
1½ tablespoons oil
1 teaspoon sugar
Salt

Fry onion almost crisp. Add the combined vinegar, water, sugar, olives, salt and simmer 5 minutes. Add the spinach, tomato, corn and cover the pan. Simmer about 15 minutes. Serve with mashed potato.

6. EGG STEW

5–6 quartered hard eggs
1½ cups stock
½ cup top milk
¼ cup chopped green onions
1½ tablespoons flour
1½ tablespoons melted margarine
2 teaspoons chopped parsley
¼ teaspoon lemon juice
Seasoning

In a double boiler blend the margarine and flour. Gradually add the stock, stirring till smooth. Add the onion, parsley, seasoning and cook 5 minutes. Add the top milk, lemon juice and egg pieces and heat well. Serve with rice or noodles.

7. HARICOT AND CELERY STEW

1 tin haricot beans
1½ tablespoons tomato sauce
1½ tablespoons hot water
2 tablespoons oil
1 chopped onion
1 chopped celery stick
2 teaspoons chopped parsley
Seasoning

Fry onion soft in 1 tablespoon oil. Add the beans and the rest of the oil. Add the combined tomato sauce and hot water and the seasoning. Simmer 15–20 minutes and place the mixture in a serving dish. Sprinkle it with the parsley.

8. LENTIL AND RICE STEW

1 cup soaked cooked lentils
1½ cups cooked rice
½ cup sliced mushrooms
¼ cup grated cheese
2 chopped hard eggs
Enriched mashed potato
2 skinned chopped tomatoes
1 chopped onion
2 tablespoons margarine
1 teaspoon mixed herbs
Seasoning
Stock

Fry the onion and mushrooms soft. Add the tomato and cook 5 minutes. Add about 1 cup of stock, the lentils, rice, egg, herbs and seasoning. Simmer 6–7 minutes and remove the pan from the fire. Add the cheese and stir till it melts. Place the mixture on the centre of a round oven dish. Around it place a ring of enriched mashed potato. Bake until the potato becomes tipped with gold in a 400°F. oven.

(3–4 people)

Enriched mashed potato:

2 cups warm mashed potato

1–2 beaten eggs

2 tablespoons hot milk

1½ tablespoons margarine

   Combine the ingredients and beat smooth.

9. MOLASSES AND BEAN STEW

1 tin baked beans

¾ cup warm water

1 tablespoon dark molasses

Scone dough

1 teaspoon made mustard

1 teaspoon lemon juice

½ teaspoon lemon rind

1 teaspoon Worcester sauce *or* soya sauce

Combine the hot water, molasses, mustard, lemon juice and rind, Worcester sauce and heat the mixture. Place it in a deep oven dish and bake it for about 10 minutes. Remove the dish from the oven and on the mixture place suitable blobs of the scone dough. Return the dish to the oven and bake until the scones become golden.

10. MUSHROOM AND POTATO STEW

1½ cups half boiled sliced potatoes

1 cup sliced fried mushrooms

½ cup yoghurt

1 chopped onion

2 tablespoons margarine

2 teaspoons chopped parsley

1 bayleaf

Seasoning

In half the margarine fry the potato slices a little. Remove them from the pan and in it place the onion and mushrooms. Fry them 5 minutes. Add the yoghurt, parsley, bayleaf, seasoning and the fried potato. Just cover the mixture with warm water and simmer it for 20–30 minutes. Remove the bayleaf and place the mixture in a serving dish.

11. Nut and Mushroom Stew

$1\frac{1}{2}$ cups mushroom soup
$\frac{1}{2}$ cup top milk
$\frac{1}{2}$ cup tinned sliced mushrooms
$\frac{3}{4}$ cup chopped nuts
$\frac{1}{4}$ cup sliced black olives
2 tablespoons flour
$1\frac{1}{2}$ tablespoons margarine
$1\frac{1}{2}$ tablespoons sherry
Seasoning

Heat the margarine till melted and add the flour. Stir till blended and gradually add the combined soup and milk, stirring till smooth. Add the rest of the ingredients and simmer 5 minutes. Place the mixture in a serving dish and serve with rice.
(*3–4 people*)

12. Nut and Rice Stew

1 cup raw rice
$\frac{1}{2}$ cup chopped onion
$\frac{1}{2}$ cup chopped nuts
$\frac{1}{4}$ cup chopped olives
$\frac{1}{4}$ cup chopped green pepper
$\frac{1}{4}$ cup chopped celery (optional)
2 skinned chopped tomatoes
2 cups boiling water
Seasoning

In the boiling water place the rice, onion, tomato, celery, olives, seasoning. When half cooked remove the mixture to the top of a double boiler and cook till the rice is soft. Add the nuts and place the mixture on a serving dish. Sprinkle it with the chopped green pepper.

(*3–4 people*)

13. NUT STEW

1 cup crushed nuts
½ cup dry breadcrumbs
1–2 cups stock
Mashed potato
1 chopped onion
1½ tablespoons margarine
1½ tablespoons ketchup
Croutons
seasoning

Fry the onion soft and add the nuts and breadcrumbs. Fry 2 minutes and add the ketchup and enough stock for a thick sauce, adding the seasoning. Arrange a ring of warm mashed potato on a serving dish and in the centre place the sauce. Decorate with croutons of fried bread

14. ONION SAUCE STEW

6–7 quartered hard eggs
2–3 fine chopped onions
1 cup milk
½ cup Ideal milk *or* cream
2 tablespoons margarine
2 tablespoons flour
½ teaspoon nutmeg
Seasoning

Fry onions soft, not brown. Add the flour and mix. Gradually add the combined milk and Ideal milk, stirring till smooth. Add the nutmeg and seasoning. Place the egg pieces on a serving dish and pour the sauce over.

15. POTATO AND CAULIFLOWER STEW

1½ cups peeled cooked sliced potatoes
1 cup broken cauliflower florets
½ cup cold water
2–3 tablespoons soy sauce
1½ tablespoons schmaltz or margarine
Garlic
salt

In the schmaltz fry the cauliflower pieces 5 minutes, tossing at times. Add the soy sauce and garlic salt. Cook a few minutes and add the water, stirring. Increase the heat and add the potatoes. Cook 3 minutes and reduce the heat. Cover the pan and simmer 5 minutes.

16. RICE AND MUSHROOM STEW

¾ cup sliced mushrooms
1 cup raw rice
3 cups stock
½ cup red wine
7 chopped pickled onions
¾ cup skinned tomato pieces
½ cup raw green peas
½ cup grated cheese
3 tablespoons salad oil
Seasoning

Fry the mushrooms and tomato 5 minutes and add the rice, stirring till well heated. Add the stock, red wine, peas, seasoning and cover the pan. Cook 10 to 15 minutes till the rice is tender. Remove the pan from the fire and add the cheese and pickled onions. Stir till the cheese melts.

(*3–4 people*)

17. SPINACH STEW

1 cup half cooked chopped spinach
1 skinned sliced tomato
1 tablespoon smooth peanut butter
1 chopped onion
$\frac{1}{2}$ chopped green pepper
$1\frac{1}{2}$ tablespoons oil
Seasoning

Fry the onion soft. Add the tomato and green pepper and cook 5 minutes. Add the spinach and seasoning and peanut butter. Simmer 10 minutes, stirring at times. Serve with mashed potato and gravy.

18. WALNUT AND BEAN STEW

$1\frac{1}{2}$ cups overnight soaked beans
$\frac{1}{2}$ cup crushed walnuts
$1\frac{1}{2}$ cups stock
1 large chopped onion
1 desertsspoon chopped parsley
Cayenne
salt

In the stock cook the beans and onion tender. Add the nuts, cayenne, salt and simmer about 10 minutes. Place the mixture in a serving dish and sprinkle with the parsley. Serve with potato chips.

SAVOURY DISHES

1. DRIED PEA SAVOURY

1½ cups overnight soaked peas
¾ cup breadcrumbs
½ cup chopped celery or green pepper
1 medium grated parsnip
2 tablespoon melted margarine
1 tablespoons nutbutter
1 teaspoon chopped mint
Seasoning

In a pan just cover the peas with water. Add the celery and parsnip and cook till tender. Remove the pan from the fire and mash the mixture. Add the margarine, mint, nutbutter, breadcrumbs and seasoning. If the mixture is too dry add some stock. Place this in a greased oven dish and bake 30–40 minutes in a moderate oven.

2. MILK WELSH RAREBIT

½ lb grated cheddar
1½ cups milk
1 egg
Buttered toast
2 tablespoons flour
1½ tablespoons margarine
1 teaspoon dry mustard
Salt

In the top of a double boiler place the cheese, egg, flour, margarine mustard, salt. Blend these and then gradually add the milk, stirring constantly. Now with a rotary beat the mixture till it becomes thick and creamy. Pour proper amounts on the toast *or* on buttered cream crackers. If liked sprinkle with parsley.

3. Nut and Cellery Toast

6 slices toast
1½ cups milk
½ cup chopped cashew nuts
1 tablespoon flour
½ tablespoon top milk
1½ tablespoons margarine
1 medium chopped onion
1 stick chopped celery *or* green pepper
Cayenne
Salt

Fry onion and celery soft. Sprinkle with flour, mixing, and gradually add the milk and top milk. Stir till thickened and add the nuts, cayenne, salt. Simmer a few minutes and then place proper amounts of the mixture on either buttered *or* fried toast.

4. Savoury Baby Marrows

1½ cups unpeeled thick sliced baby marrows
2 cups cooked rice
½ cup cold water
2 skinned chopped tomatoes
3 chopped spring onions
1 bayleaf
3 tablespoons oil
1 teaspoon lemon juice
½ teaspoon coriander seeds
Paprika
Garlic salt

Fry onions 3 minutes and add the tomatoes, bayleaf, coriander, paprika, garlic salt, water. Simmer 6 minutes and add the marrow slices, tossing. Cover the pan and gently cook for 20–25 minutes till tender. Add the lemon juice and pour the sauce over the rice. Serve with a green salad.
(*3–4 people*)

5. Savoury Bake

1½ cups toasted breadcrumbs
1½ cups tomato juice
¾ cup milk
2 large beaten eggs
3 tablespoons chopped onion
1 tablespoon chopped parsley
2 teaspoons thinned peanut butter
Cayenne
Seasoning

Soak the crumbs 15 minutes in the milk. Add the tomato juice, peanut butter, onion, eggs, parsley, cayenne, seasoning. Place the mixture in a greased oven dish and bake 40–50 minutes in a moderate oven.

6. Savoury Bean and Tomato Puree

2 cups soaked cooked dried beans, tomato and cheese puree
    Place the beans in an oven dish and over them pour the tomato and cheese puree. Keep in the oven till well heated.

Tomato and cheese puree:
1½ cups skinned sliced tomatoes
¾ cup grated Cheddar
1 chopped onion
1 dessertspoon brown sugar
1 teaspoon made mustard
Seasoning

Cook the tomato and onion 10 minutes and then sieve them. Add the sugar, mustard, seasoning. Remove the pan from the fire and add the cheese, stirring till melted.

7. SAVOURY FRIED BREAD

¾ inch thick trimmed bread slices
breadcrumbs
beaten egg
milk
Oil
Chopped parsley
Grated lemon rind
Mixed herbs
Nutmeg
Seasoning

Half soak the bread slices in the milk. Then dip them into the egg
and then the combined crumbs, parsley, herbs, rind, nutmeg, seasoning. Fry both sides in the hot oil. Serve with a light gravy.

8. SAVOURY MUSHROOMS AND CAULIFLOWER

1½ cups half boiled cauliflower pieces
¾ cup sliced fried mushrooms
¾ cup grated Cheddar
1 cup warm milk
1 tablespoon flour
1 tablespoon margarine
½ chopped onion
Seasoning

Place the combined cauliflower and mushrooms in a greased oven
dish. Fry the onion golden and then blend in the flour. Gradually
add the warm milk and stir till thickened. Add half the cheese and
the seasoning and stir till this melts. Pour the sauce over the cauliflower mixture. Sprinkle with the rest of the cheese and bake 20–30
minutes in a 400°F. oven.

Pancake mixture
Sauce
2 tablespoons margarine
¼ cup chopped onion
1 desertsspoon chopped parsley
1 teaspoon mixed herbs

To the pancake batter add the onion, parsley, herbs, and fry small fritters. Roll them up and place them in a warm serving dish. Pour the sauce over.

Pancake Mixture:
½ cup flour
1½ cups milk
1 large beaten egg
Seasoning

Combine the ingredients and let the mixture stand for at least an half hour before using it.

Sauce:
1½ cups milk
¼ cup top milk
½ cup grated cheese
1 tablespoon margarine
1 teaspoon made mustard
Seasoning

In the top of a double boiler place the margarine – blend in the flour. Gradually add the warm milk and stir till smooth. Remove the pan from the fire. Add the cheese and stir till melted.

10. Savoury Potato with Peanut Butter

2 cups cooked sliced potatoes
3 chopped hard eggs
1 large chopped onion
3 cups rather thin white sauce
1½ tablespoons margarine
3 teaspoons peanut butter
Yellow colouring
Seasoning

Fry the onion soft and add the combined white sauce, peanut butter, seasoning and colouring. Place the potatoes in a warm serving dish and pour the sauce over. Sprinkle with the chopped egg. (*3–4 people*)

11. Savoury Spinach Roll

2 cups cooked Chopped spinach
1½ cups grated cheddar
1 cup yoghurt *or* sour milk
1 cup white sauce
3 eggs
Filling
Cheese sauce
Seasoning

Combine the spinach, white sauce, yoghurt, cheese, beaten yolks, stiff eggwhites and place the mixture in a greased Swiss roll tin. Bake it for about 20 minutes in a moderate oven and then turn it out on a damp cloth. Cover it with a layer of filling and roll up as for a Swiss Roll. Reheat it and serve with the cheese sauce.

Filling:
$\frac{3}{4}$ cup chopped nuts
3 tablespoons tomato sauce
$\frac{1}{2}$ tablespoon margarine
Seasoning
Combine the ingredients.

Cheese Sauce:
A white sauce with cheese added
(*3–4 people*)

PIE DISHES

1. BEAN AND MUSHROOM PIE

Pie dish lined with pastry
$\frac{1}{2}$ cup tinned haricots
$\frac{1}{2}$ cup sliced mushrooms
$\frac{1}{4}$ cup bean stock
$\frac{1}{4}$ cup breadcrumbs
1 medium cooked mashed onion
1 tablespoon oil
$\frac{1}{2}$ tablespoon margarine
$\frac{1}{2}$ teaspoon mixed herbs
Seasoning

Mash the beans with the margarine and seasoning and mash the onion also with some of the margarine. To each mash add a dash of mixed herbs. On the pastry place a layer of breadcrumbs and cover it with fried mushrooms and then of mashed beans and then of onion. Repeat the layers till the dish is full. Pour over the bean stock. Cover the pie with pastry and gash the top decoratively. Bake 30 to 40 minutes in a moderate oven.
(*3–4 people*)

2. BRINJAL PIE

1 peeled Brinjal slices
$1\frac{1}{4}$ cups milk and top milk
1 tin tomato puree
2 large beaten eggs
4 tablespoons grated cheese
4 tablespoons breadcrumbs
2 tablespoons margarine
Flour
seasoning

Sprinkle the brinjal slices with salt and let them stand for half an hour. Then dry the slices, dip them into combined flour and seasoning and fry them golden. Drain and place them in a pie dish. Pour over the combined eggs, milk, seasoning and bake 30–40 minutes in a 325°F. oven. Then over the cooked custard pour over the warmed tomato puree. Sprinkle with combined crumbs and cheese. Dot with margarine and grill golden.

(4–5 people)

3. EGG PIE

$1\frac{1}{2}$ to 2 cups enriched mashed potato
The number of bread fingers to match the dish
$\frac{1}{2}$–1 cup brown gravy
1 tablespoon margarine
1 dessertspoon chopped parsley
3 hard eggs
2 raw eggs
Paprika
Salt

In the centre of a piedish place a layer of mashed potato. On top of it place a layer of the combined mashed hard egg yolks, 2 raw egg yolks, paprika and seasoning. Around this place the combined chopped hard egg whites, parsley and the gravy. Beat the remaining 1 raw eggyolk and the 3 raw egg whites together and dip the bread fingers in it. Arrange them on the pie. Sprinkle paprika and bake golden in a moderate oven.

(3- 4 people)

4. Egg and Tomato Pie

3 skinned sliced tomatoes
3 half boiled sliced onions
$\frac{1}{2}$ cup brown breadcrumbs
$\frac{1}{2}$ cup grated cheese
2 sliced hard eggs
1$\frac{1}{2}$ tablespoons margarine
1$\frac{1}{2}$ teaspoons sugar
Sauce
Salt

Cover the base of a greased piedish with tomato slices. Sprinkle them with sugar and salt. Over them place the onion slices and on top of them place the hard egg slices. Pour the sauce over and on it sprinkle a layer of combined crumbs and cheese. Dot well with margarine and bake golden in a 375°F. oven.

Sauce:
1$\frac{1}{2}$ tablespoons flour
1$\frac{1}{2}$ tablespoons margarine
1$\frac{1}{2}$ cups milk
$\frac{1}{4}$ cup grated cheese
1 teaspoon made mustard
Salt

With the margarine, flour, milk, salt, make a white sauce. Remove the pan from the fire and add the mustard and cheese, stirring till melted.

5. POTATO PIE

1½ cups cooked mashed potato
3 tablespoons holsum or margarine
3 tablespoons flour
2 beaten eggs
Filling
Seasoning
1 medium chopped onion

Grate the holsum into the mashed potato. Add the flour, onion, beaten egg, seasoning, and roll into a round for the greased pie dish into which place it carefully. Pour in the filling and bake 30–40 minutes in a moderate oven.

Filling:
1 chopped fried onion
3 beaten eggs
1½ cups milk
½ cup grated cheese
1 dessertspoon chopped parsley
Seasoning
Combine the ingredients.

EXTRA MEATLESS DISHES

1. Avocado Omelette

1 cup mashed avocado
2 beaten eggs
1 tablespoon oil
1½ teaspoons chopped dills
1½ teaspoons chopped parsley
1 teaspoon lemon juice
Seasoning

Combine the avocado, eggs, seasoning and beat until smooth and light. Pour this into a pan with heated oil and cook as for an omelette. Slide it to a warm serving dish. Sprinkle with the dill, parsley, lemon juice, and fold the omelette over.
(*2 people*)

2. Batter Tomatoes

3 skinned thickly sliced tomatoes
1 cup fritter batter
½ cup grated cheese
½ cup chopped onion
2 teaspoons sugar
Oil
Salt

Combine the batter, cheese, onion, salt. Sprinkle the tomato slices with sugar and then dip them well coated in the enriched batter. Fry them golden both sides and serve them with a nut dish.

3. Cauliflower Egg Scramble

1½ cups half cooked cauliflower florets
4 beaten eggs
1 chopped onion
1½ tablespoons margarine
½ teaspoon caraway seeds *or* herbs
Seasoning

Fry the onion golden. Add the cauliflower, caraway, seasoning and cook 5 minutes, tossing at times. Pour eggs over and stir till lightly cooked and wet. Serve with potato chips.

4. Creamed Kohl Rabi

1½ cups peeled cubed kohlrabis
1½ cups rather thin white sauce
½ cup grated cheese
2 tablespoons vinegar
1 large beaten egg
Paprika
Salt

Pour the vinegar over the kohl rabi and let it stand for 1 hour tossing it at times. Rinse the cubes and cook them uncovered in water for 25–30 minutes. Drain and place them in a serving dish heated. Pour over the white sauce enriched in a double boiler with the egg. Sprinkle with paprika.

5. Carrot Macaroni

2 cups broken macaroni
1 cup thin sliced carrots
½ cup grated cheese
6 sugared and salted, fried tomato halves
1½ tablespoons margarine
Seasoning

Sprinkle the carrots with seasoning and fry them about 10 minutes in the margarine. Cook the macaroni and add the fried carrots and the cheese. Place the mixture on a warm serving dish and surround it with the fried tomato halves.
(*3–4 people*)

6. Mushroom Rice

2 cups cooked rice
1 cup tinned peas
$\frac{3}{4}$ cup chopped onion
$\frac{1}{2}$ cup sliced mushrooms
$\frac{1}{2}$ cup chopped fried nuts
$\frac{1}{4}$ cup chopped celery *or* green pepper
$2\frac{1}{2}$ tablespoons margarine
3 beaten eggs and a little water
Seasoning

Fry the onion, mushrooms and celery soft. Add the peas, seasoning, and mix. Then add the rice and toss the mixture constantly to keep it from burning. When heated pour the eggs and water liquid over and stir it gently for about 3 minutes. Place the mixture in a warm serving dish and sprinkle it with the fried nuts.
(*3-4 people*)

7. Parsnip Cakes

$1\frac{1}{2}$ cups boiled mashed parsnips
$\frac{3}{4}$ cup chopped nuts
1 large beaten egg
2 tablespoons oil
1 tablespoon flour
1 tablespoon melted margarine
1 tablespoon chopped parsley
Cayenne
Salt

Combine the parsnip, margarine, nuts, cayenne, salt and shape into cakes. Dip them into the egg and then into flour and fry them golden. Serve with gravy and fried tomatoes.

8. PARSNIP ROLLS

1¼ cups cooked mashed parsnips
½ cup cooked mashed potatoes
1 chopped onion
1 beaten egg
1 tablespoon chopped parsley
1 tablespoon Worcester *or* soy sauce
Breadcrumbs *or* flour
Oil *or* margarine
Seasoning

Fry the onion and add all *but* the flour *or* crumbs and the oil. With floured hands shape small rolls and dip into and cover them with crumbs. Fry them golden.

9. SPINACH RING

2½ cups cooked chopped spinach
1¾ cups enriched white sauce
5 quartered hard eggs
½ cup grated cheese
3 tablespoons top milk
Seasoning

In the top of a double boiler place the spinach, half cup white sauce, cheese, seasoning. Cook till the cheese melts and then with it make a ring around the edge of a pie dish. In the centre place the combined eggs, rest of the white sauce, top milk and some seasoning. Serve with mashed potato.

10. Tomato Sauce Macaroni

$2\frac{1}{2}$ cups cooked macaroni pieces
$\frac{1}{4}$ cup stoned chopped olives
$\frac{1}{4}$ cup tomato sauce
1 tablespoon capers
3 tablespoons top milk
Seasoning

Combine the tomato sauce and top milk and add the olives, capers, seasoning. Pour it over the macaroni and toss till well mixed.

MEATLESS SOUPS

1. COLD CUCUMBER SOUP

3 medium peeled cucumbers
3 cups vegetable stock
1 cup yoghurt
2½ teaspoons chopped parsley *or* 2½ teaspoons fresh mixed herbs
    or 2½ chopped dill *or* chives
Seasonings

From the cucumbers remove the seeds. Dice them and add them to the stock which has been heated. Boil 10 minutes till soft and press the cucumbers through a sieve. Let the liquid cool and add the yoghurt and seasonings. Chill and then garnish with any of the extras given later.

2. CURRY SOUP

4 cups vegetable stock
1 cup soaked beans
1 chopped onion
1½ tablespoons flour
3 teaspoons curry powder
3 cloves
1 bayleaf
seasoning
Oil

Drain the beans and cook them soft with the stock, cloves and bayleaf. Remove the cloves and bayleaf and sieve the rest of the mixture. Fry the onion golden and add the flour, curry powder, seasoning, mixing well. Add this to the soup and stir till thickened.
(*3–4 people*)

3. Cabbage Soup

3 cups vegetable stock
2 cups shredded cabbage
1 cup diced potato
$\frac{1}{2}$ cup Ideal or top milk
$2\frac{1}{2}$ tablespoons oil
1 chopped onion
1 teaspoon mixed herbs *or* paprika
Seasoning

Fry the onion, potato and cabbage for 10 minutes, tossing often. Add the stock and seasoning and cook for half an hour. Press the mixture through a sieve. Reheat it and add the top milk. Serve it sprinkled with the herbs *or* paprika.

4. Clear Soup with Noodles

2 cups potato water
1 cup bean water
$\frac{1}{2}$ cup noodles
$\frac{1}{4}$ cup chopped onion
1 teaspoon soy sauce *or* $\frac{1}{2}$ teaspoon marmite *or* $\frac{1}{2}$ cup vegemite
Seasoning

Add the soy sauce to the combined potato and bean waters. Heat and add the onion. Cook until it is soft and then strain. Add the noodles and cook till soft. Add the seasoning.

5. Green Pea Soup

1½ cups soaked cooked dried green peas
2 cups vegetable stock
1 chopped onion
3 tablespoons top *or* Ideal milk
½ teaspoon chopped mint
1 teaspoon brown sugar
¼ cup grated cheese
Seasoning

Heat the stock and add the peas, onion, and cook till soft. Rub the mixture through a sieve. Reheat it and add the top milk, brown sugar, seasoning. Bring this to the boil and remove the soup to a serving dish. Sprinkle it with the combined mint and cheese.

6. Haricot Soup

1 cup overnight soaked haricots
2½ cups thin white sauce
1 chopped onion
1 teaspoon vinegar
½ teaspoon thyme
1 bayleaf
Seasoning

Cook the beans soft in the water in which they were soaked. Add the onion, bayleaf, thyme, seasoning. Cook a few minutes and remove from the fire. Sieve the mixture and add the white sauce and if liked, the vinegar.

7. LENTIL AND ASPARAGUS SOUP

1½ cups soaked, cooked, sieved lentil puree
1 small tin asparagus pieces and the asparagus water
2½ cups vegetable stock
2 beaten egg yolks
1 cup Ideal *or* top milk
Seasoning

Simmer the stock, lentil puree, asparagus water for 10 minutes. Remove the pan from the fire and let the contents cool. Add the combined yolks and top milk, stirring. Heat for 6 to 7 minutes but *do not boil*. Place the asparagus pieces in a warm serving dish and pour the soup over.
(*3–4 people*)

8. LENTIL SOUP

2 cups overnight soaked lentils
3 cups water
½ cup milk
1½ tablespoons margarine
1½ tablespoons flour
½ teaspoon nutmeg
1 large chopped onion
Seasoning

Fry the onion golden and add the drained lentils and the water. Cook till the lentils are soft and sieve the mixture. Return it to the saucepan and thicken it with a paste of flour and milk, stirring well. Add the seasoning, Cook a few minutes.

9. POTATO AND CABBAGE SOUP

2 cups chopped raw potatoes
1 cup chopped cabbage
1 large sliced onion
3 cups hot water
2 tablespoons oil
Seasoning

In a saucepan fry the onion golden. Add the potato and cabbage and fry them for 5 minutes, tossing. Add the hot water and simmer the mixture until it thickens to one's liking, stirring at times. Add the seasoning

10. POTATO AND PEA SOUP

1½ cups peeled diced potatoes
¾ cup green peas
3 cups skim milk
1 small chopped onion
2 tablespoons margarine
1 tablespoon flour
1 dessertspoon chopped parsley
Seasoning

In a saucepan place the potato, peas, onion and cover them with 1 inch of water. Boil them till they are tender and then add the skim milk. Bring this to the boil and then simmer for five minutes. In a frying pan heat the flour till it turns pale golden. Add the margarine and blend the mixture, stirring till it browns but does not burn. Add this to the soup, stirring till the soup thickens a little. Add the seasoning and when ready to serve sprinkle the soup with parsley.

11. POTATO SOUP

3 medium cooked potatoes
3 cups milk
Chopped parsley *or* mixed herbs
Cayenne
2 tablespoons chopped onion
2 tablespoons melted margarine
1½ tablespoons flour
Seasoning

Rub the potatoes through a sieve. Bring to the boil the milk and onion. Add it to the sieved potato, beating well. Blend the melted margarine and flour, and to it add 2 tablespoons of the milk and onion mixture. Gradually stir it into the liquid. Add the cayenne and seasoning and boil for 5 minutes. When about to serve sprinkle it with parsley *or* mixed herbs.

12. RICE SOUP

4 cups stock
1½ cups rice
1 cup grated cheese
1 chopped onion
2½ tablespoons margarine
½ teaspoon nutmeg
½ teaspoon saffron
Seasoning

In 1 tablespoon margarine fry the onion soft. Add the stock, rice, saffron and simmer for 30 minutes, adding extra stock if needed. Remove the pan from the fire and add the rest of the margarine, the cheese, nutmeg and seasoning, stirring till the cheese melts. Reheat but *do not boil*.

13. Sago and Marmite Soup

3 cups stock *or* water
2 tablespoons tapioca *or* fine sago
Some top milk if wished
1 large grated carrot
1 medium chopped onion
1 dessertspoon marmite
2 teaspoons chopped parsley

Simmer the stock, carrot, onion, parsley for 10 minutes. Add the tapioca *or* sago and cook till it becomes soft (50–60 minutes). If clear soup is wanted strain the liquid and add the marmite, stirring. If not then strain the soup and add as much of the sago and vegetables as wanted. Then add the top milk it wished.
(*4–5 people*)

14. Split Pea Soup

1½ cups overnight soaked green split peas
2 cups stock *or* water
½ cup thick skim milk
1 large grated carrot
1 medium chopped onion
1 bayleaf
½ teaspoon celery salt
½ teaspoon garlic salt
½ teaspoon mixed herbs (optional)

Combine the ingredients and cook till they are soft. Remove the bayleaf and press the mixture through a sieve and heat again. It might be better to add the skim milk at the end.

15. Tomato Soup

1 cup rice
3–4 skinned, cooked sieved tomatoes
3 cups stock *or* water
1½ tablespoons margarine
½ tablespoon vinegar
1 dessertspoon sugar
1½ tablespoons grated cheese
Cayenne
Salt

Bring the stock to the boil and add the rice and margarine. Cook till soft and add the tomato, vinegar, sugar, cayenne, salt. Cook another 5 minutes and serve with sprinkled on cheese.
(*3–4 people*)

16. Vegetable Soup

3 cups stock
2 cups skim milk
¾ cup cubed potatoes
¼ cup cubed carrots
¼ cup cubed kohl rabi *or* turnip
¼ cup cubed beetroot
¼ cup skinned chopped tomato
1 tablespoon chopped chives
1 dessertspoon chopped parsley
1½ tablespoons flour
1 tablespoon margarine *or* butter
Seasoning

To boiling water add the cubed potato, carrot, beetroot, chopped tomato. Cook till they are tender. Make a paste with the flour and a little milk and to it add the rest of the milk. Gradually add this to the soup and stir till thickened. Then add the margarine, chives, parsley, seasoning. Cook 10 minutes more and serve with soup croutons.
(*3–4 people*)

ADDITIONS FOR SOUP

1. CARAWAY FINGERS FOR SOUP

4 slices trimmed white or brown bread
Margarine or butter
Caraway seeds

Butter one side of the slices and sprinkle them with caraway seeds. Place them on a greased oven sheet and grill them golden. Cut the toasted slices into fingers and serve with soup.

2. GARLIC BREAD CUBES

2 cups bread cubes
¼ cup melted margarine
1½ tablespoons garlic salt

Cream the margarine and add the cubes, rolling them till they are covered with margarine and added garlic salt. Place them on a greased oven sheet and bake them in a 375°F. oven, turning them once till they are golden all over.

3. PANCAKE SHREDS

1 cup skim milk
2 beaten eggs
1 cup grated cheese
1½ tablespoons flour
1 tablespoon margarine
½ tablespoon chopped parsley
Seasoning

Combine the ingredients and place the mixture in a well greased frying pan. Fry golden both sides and remove the pan from the fire. Cut the pancake or pancakes into shreds and serve with the soup.

4. Savoury Cubes for Soup

1 cup bread cubes
Grated cheese
1 tablespoon Soy sauce with 1 tablespoon water
or
1 tablespoon Worcester sauce with 1 tablespoon water

Dip the bread cubes quickly in and out of the liquid and then roll them in the cheese. Place them on a greased oven sheet and bake them for 5 minutes till golden in a 450°F. oven.

5. Vegetable Stock for Soup

Any water used for cooking vegetables contains good mineral salts and should be used when possible for ordinary water.

GRAVIES

1. Brown Colouring for Gravy

2 cups water
¾ cup sugar
Salt

Use an old pan for this as it can discolour a new one. In the pan
place the sugar and heat it to almost burning while stirring. Add
the water and salt and mix briskly while cooking for 5 minutes.
Remove this from the fire. Let cool and bottle. It keeps well in the
refrigerator and can be used to colour gravies, sauces and soups.

2. Chinese Gravy

2 cups thin hot soup or stock
Seasoning
1 dessertspoon maizena or flour
1½ teaspoons marmite *or* soy sauce
1 teaspoon dark molasses

Make a paste of maizena and 3 tablespoons soup. Add the soy
sauce and molasses, stirring over the fire. Gradually add the hot
soup *or* stock and heat, cooking till thickened.

3. Claret Gravy

1 cup light red wine
½ cup marmite water
1 tablespoon maizena
½ tablespoon horse radish
¼ tablespoon lemon juice, or less
1 tablespoon cold water
1½ teaspoons sugar
Paprika
Salt

Bring to boiling point the marmite water, red wine, horse radish, lemon juice, sugar, paprika, seasoning. Stir gradually into it a paste of maizena and water. Stir till thickened.

4. CURRY GRAVY

3 cups stock *or* water
2 tablespoons flour
2 tablespoons margarine
2–3 teaspoons curry powder
1 teaspoon marmite
$\frac{1}{2}$ teaspoon celery seed *or* mixed herbs

Heat the margarine and add the combined flour and curry powder Cook till well golden and gradually add the stock, stirring till thickened. Add the marmite, flavouring and seasoning.

5. EASY BROWN GRAVY

$1\frac{1}{2}$ cups stock
1 chopped onion
$1\frac{1}{2}$ tablespoons flour
$1\frac{1}{2}$ tablespoons oil
1 teaspoon marmite
1 teaspoon maggi sauce
$\frac{1}{4}$ teaspoon tobasco

Fry the onion golden and add the flour. Cook golden without burning. Gradually add the combined stock, marmite, tobasco, maggi sauce. Over a gentle heat stir till the sauce thickens.

6. Mushroom Gravy

¾ cup raw sliced mushrooms
½ cup cold water
2 tablespoons chopped onion
2 tablespoons Soy sauce
2 tablespoons yoghurt
1½ tablespoons oil
Garlic salt

In the oil fry the onion and mushrooms gently for 5 minutes. Increase the heat and add the soy sauce and cook till the mixture becomes richly brown. Add the water, stirring and cook 2 minutes. Add the yoghurt, mixing, and cook another 2 minutes. A nice gravy for potatoes or macaroni.

7. Onion Gravy

1 large thin sliced onion
1–2 tablespoons flour
1 tablespoons sugar
1½ tablespoons margarine
1½ teaspoons vinegar
Vegetable stock
Seasoning

In the margarine swiftly brown the sugar. Add the onion and cook 3 minutes. Add the flour, mixing, and then gradually add enough stock for the thickness of gravy you want. Stir well and simmer for 10–15 minutes. Remove the pan from the fire. Add the vinegar and seasoning and reheat the gravy.

8. Sherry Gravy

2 cups vegetable stock
1 tablespoon sherry
$\frac{1}{2}$ tablespoon mushroom ketchup
2–2$\frac{1}{2}$ teaspoons maizena
1 teaspoon marmite
2 teaspoons chopped nuts (optional)

Make a paste of the maizena and ketchup. To it gradually add the warm stock, stirring till smooth. Add the sherry, marmite and the nuts and simmer 5 minutes.

9. Vegetable Brown Gravy

2 cups stock *or* water
$\frac{1}{2}$ grated carrot
$\frac{1}{2}$ grated turnip
$\frac{1}{2}$ chopped onion
1$\frac{1}{2}$ tablespoons margarine
2 teaspoons vinegar *or* lemon juice
1 teaspoon Worcester *or* other sauce
1 teaspoon sugar
1 teaspoon chopped parsley
Seasoning

Fry the onion, carrot, turnip darkish brown. Sprinkle with flour and gradually add the stock, stirring till the mixture thickens. Add the vinegar, sugar, parsley, seasoning and simmer 10–15 minutes. Strain the mixture and then add the Worcester sauce and reheat.

UNSWEET SAUCES

1. BREAD AND MAYONNAISE SAUCE

2 trimmed slices bread
Garlic salt
1 cup mayonnaise
$\frac{3}{4}$ cup milk

Pour the milk on the bread and let it soak in for 5 minutes. Then squeeze out the milk and to the bread add the garlic salt. Add the mayonnaise and mix well. Use this for salads.

2. CHEESE SAUCE

$1\frac{1}{2}$ cups milk
1 cup grated cheese
$1\frac{1}{2}$ tablespoons flour
$1\frac{1}{2}$ tablespoons melted margarine
Seasoning

In the top of a double boiler blend the margarine and flour. Gradually add the milk and stir till thickened. Add the cheese and stir till it melts. Add the seasoning.

3. CURRY SAUCE

2 cups stock *or* water
1 medium chopped onion
1 medium chopped apple
1 chopped banana
1 tablespoon flour
1½ tablespoons margarine
1 dessertspoon vinegar *or* lemon juice
1 dessertspoon curry powder
1 dessertspoon chutney
1 dessertspoon apricot jam
1 dessertspoon chopped raisins
Seasoning

Fry the onion, apple and banana 5 minutes. Add the combined flour and curry powder, mixing. Gradually add the stock, stirring till thickened. Add the rest of the ingredients and simmer for 5 minutes.

4. CURRY SALAD SAUCE

1½ cups sour cream *or* yoghurt
1 dessertspoon lemon juice
1 dessertspoon horseradish
1 dessertspoon sugar
1 teaspoon made mustard
1 teaspoon grated lemon rind
2 teaspoons curry powder
Garlic salt

Combine the ingredients, tossing well.

5. Chinese Sweet Sour Sauce

2 tablespoons vinegar
6 tablespoons stock *or* water
1 tablespoons flour
1½ tablespoons chopped onion *or* pickles
1 dessertspoon sugar
1 teaspoon marmite *or* Worcester sauce
Seasoning

Make a thin smooth paste with the flour, vinegar, sugar, water, Worcester sauce, seasoning. Heat gently till the mixture boils, stirring. Add the onion and simmer 5 minutes. Nice with cooked green beans or broccoli.

6. Green Sauce

½ cup chopped spinach leaves
½ cup chopped parsley
½ cup chopped walnuts
½ cup salad oil
1 teaspoon crushed peppercorns
1 teaspoon Basil
1 teaspoon garlic salt

Crush all the ingredients but the oil as fine as possible *or* run them through a blender. Then add the oil, mixing well. Place the sauce in a jar and keep it in the refrigerator till wanted.

7. Herb Sauce ✓

1½ cups skim milk
1½–2 tablespoons margarine
1½ tablespoons flour
1 tablespoon chopped onion
1 teaspoon made mustard
1 teaspoon mixed herbs
Garlic Salt
Pepper

Fry the onion soft and add the flour, mixing. Gradually add the milk and stir till thickened. Add the mustard, herbs, seasoning and simmer 5 minutes

8. Horseradish Sauce

½ cup Ideal *or* top milk
1 beaten egg yolk
1½ tablespoons horseradish
1 teaspoon made mustard
1 teaspoon vinegar
1 teaspoon sugar
Salt

Combine the ingredients and beat the mixture till it becomes thick and creamy.

9. Mint Salad Sauce

1 skinned chopped tomato
1 medium chopped onion
1 tablespoon chopped mint leaves
1 cup salad cream
Dash of Tobasco
1 teaspoon sugar
Salt

Combine the ingredients and if the mixture is too thick add a little white wine and extra sugar. If both the salad cream and wine are omitted the mixture can be used as a chutney.

10. MUSTARD SAUCE

1 cup Ideal *or* top milk
2 beaten eggs
1 dessertspoon margarine
Salt
½ tablespoon flour
½ tablespoon wine or vinegar
1 teaspoon made mustard
1 teaspoon sugar

Place all the ingredients but the margarine in the top of a double boiler. With a rotary beat till it thickens. Remove the pan from the fire and beat 3 minutes longer. Add the margarine and stir it till it melts. A nice sauce for asparagus or hard eggs.

11. NUTTY SALAD SAUCE

1 cup mayonnaise
¼ cup ketchup
1 teaspoon sugar
1 tablespoon chopped olives
2 tablespoons chopped chives
1 tablespoon crushed roasted peanuts
Seasoning

Combine the ingredients, mixing well. If too thick add a little white wine and a little extra sugar.

12. Onion Sauce

1 cup dark stock
3 medium sliced onions
2 tablespoons margarine
1 tablespoon flour
½ tablespoon vinegar
1 teaspoon sugar
Salt

Melt the margarine and brown the sugar in it. Add the onion and fry it till almost tender. Add the flour, mixing. Gradually add the liquids and stir till the mixture thickens. Add the salt and simmer 5 minutes.

13. Rich Cheese Sauce

1½ cups milk and water
1 tablespoon flour
1 tablespoon margarine
¾ cup grated cheese
2 teaspoons chopped onion
1 teaspoon dry mustard
½ teaspoon Worcester sauce
Seasoning

Make a white sauce with the combined flour, mustard, seasoning, the margarine and the milk and water. Add the onion and simmer 6–7 minutes. Add the Worcester sauce and then the cheese, stirring till it melts.

14. Red Wine Sauce

1¼ cups red wine
3–4 tablespoons margarine
1 dessertspoon chopped shallots
1½ teaspoons sugar
Seasoning

Boil the wine until it is half reduced. Add the rest of the ingredients and with a rotary beat till a creamy red butter is obtained. Nice for savoury dishes.

15. Sauce for Omelette Centre

1 cup skim milk
2 tablespoons chopped onion
$\frac{3}{4}$ tablespoon flour
1 tablespoon margarine
$\frac{1}{2}$ tablespoon curry powder
$1\frac{1}{2}$ teaspoons chutney
Salt

Fry the onion soft and add the combined flour, curry powder, seasoning, mixing. Gradually add the milk and stir till thickened. Add the rest of the ingredients and simmer 5 minutes. Add more milk if a thinner sauce is wanted.

16. Special Sauce

$\frac{1}{4}$ cup thin soup
$\frac{1}{2}$ cup stock
$\frac{1}{2}$ cup white wine
3–4 tablespoons breadcrumbs
Nutmeg to taste
1 dessertspoon margarine
1 dessertspoon chopped shallots
2 teaspoons chopped parsley
1 teaspoon lemon juice
Garlic salt

Combine the wine, shallot, parsley and cook till half reduced. Add the soup, breadcrumbs, margarine, stock and reduce by half again. Add the lemon juice.

17. SWEET SOUR SAUCE No 1

1 cup vinegar
½ tablespoon flour *or* maizena
1 beaten egg
1 dessertspoon margarine
2 teaspoons sugar
Salt

Place all but the margarine in the top of a double boiler. Without boiling cook till the mixture thickens, stirring. Remove the pan from the fire and add the margarine. Stir till melted.

18. SWEET SOUR SAUCE No 2

1 cup stock *or* water
1 tablespoon flour
½ tablespoon vinegar
1–2 teaspoons Worcester, marmite *or* other sauce
2 teaspoons chopped pickles
2 teaspoons sugar
Seasoning

In the top of a double boiler place the vinegar, sugar, Worcester sauce, seasoning. Add a paste made with the flour and stock and cook, stirring till thickened. Add the pickle and cook 5 minutes more. This sauce is nice with cooked green beans or broccoli.

19. SAUCE WITH OLIVES

¾ cup fine chopped black olives
¼ cup grated cheese
2–3 tablespoons salad oil
1 tablespoon lemon juice
1 teaspoon sugar

Pound the olives and cheese smooth. Drop by drop add the oil till the mixture begins to thicken. Add the lemon juice and sugar, mixing well. It is a tasty sauce for new potatoes, hard boiled eggs or as a noodle dressing if heated. Nice also for an omelette filling.

20. SAUCE WITH GROUND ALMONDS AND LEMON JUICE

$\frac{1}{2}$ cup blanched pounded almonds
$\frac{1}{4}$ cup salad oil
1 tablespoon lemon juice
1 teaspoon sugar
Garlic salt

Combine the almonds, lemon juice, sugar, garlic salt and pound it to a creamy paste. Drop by drop add the oil, beating constantly till the colour of the mixture becomes pale beige. Store in the refrigerator. Delicious with new potatoes, baby carrots, tender green beans, beetroot, cauliflower, and a tasty filling for avocado pear.

21. SPECIAL SAUCE FOR SPAGHETTI

1 cup dry red wine
$\frac{1}{4}$ cup skinned, seeded, chopped tomato
2 tablespoons fine chopped onion
$1\frac{1}{2}$ tablespoons fine chopped black olives
1 tablespoon fine chopped celery leaves *or* green pepper
2 teaspoons sugar
$\frac{1}{2}$ teaspoon mixed herbs
Garlic salt

Fry onion soft and add the tomato, olives, celery, sugar, herbs, garlic salt and gently simmer for 10 minutes. Add the wine and bring the mixture to the boil. Lessen the heat and simmer gently for 20 minutes, stirring at times. Sieve the sauce, pour it over the warm spaghetti.

BATTER, MAYONNAISE, SALAD DRESSING

1. Condensed Milk Mayonnaise

½ cup sweet condensed milk
¼ cup lemon juice
¼ cup salad oil
2 egg yolks
2 teaspoons dry mustard
Salt

Blend the ingredients and store in the refrigerator.

2. Cooked Mayonnaise

1½ cups water
¼ cup lemon juice
¼ cup salad oil
1 egg
2–3 tablespoons maizena
1 tablespoon sugar
Paprika
Salt

In a deep bowl place the egg, sugar, lemon juice, oil, seasonings and *do not stir*. With a little water make a paste with the maizena. Bring the rest of the water to the boil and add the maizena paste, stirring till thickened. Pour this briskly into the mixture in the bowl and with a rotary beat it smooth.

BATTER

1. FRITTER BATTER

1 cup flour
1 plus cups milk
1 beaten egg
2 teaspoons baking powder
Salt

Gradually add the combined egg and milk to the sifted dry ingredients and stir till smooth.

2. BATTER FOR VEGETABLES

1 cup milk
$\frac{1}{4}$ cup flour
1 beaten egg
1 tablespoon margarine *or* salad oil
Salt

Gradually add the combined milk and egg to the sifted dry ingredients, beating well. Add the oil and beat smooth with a rotary. If not thick enough add extra flour. A good batter in which to dip various vegetable pieces, even brinjals. After dipping fry the vegetable pieces in deepish hot oil.

3. PANCAKE BATTER

$1\frac{1}{2}$ cups milk
2 eggs
3–4 tablespoons flour
$1\frac{1}{2}$ tablespoons salad oil
Salt

Sieve the flour and salt and in it make a well. Drop in the eggs and add the oil. Mix and then gradually add the milk. Stir for a smooth batter. Let stand for half an hour before using.

SALAD DRESSINGS

1. French Salad Dressing

½ cup salad oil
2 teaspoons sugar
2 tablespoons lemon juice *or* 1 tablespoon vinegar
Salt

Combine the ingredients in a jar and shake them till well mixed.
Chill.

2. Nice Salad Dressing

½ plus cups salad oil
4 tablespoons lemon *or* grape juice
1–1½ teaspoons sugar
½ teaspoon dry mustard
Garlic salt

Place all the ingredients in a jar and shake for at least 10 minutes.
Store in the refrigerator and always shake before using.

3. Rochfort Dressing

½ cup crumbled Rochfort cheese
4 tablespoons salad oil
2 tablespoons vinegar
3 tablespoons milk or top milk
1 teaspoon made mustard
1 teaspoon Worcester sauce
Seasoning

In a bowl placed over crushed ice, combine the cheese, mustard,
Worcester sauce, seasoning and mix them. Alternately add the
vinegar and oil, beating very well.

4. Savoury Dressing

4½ tablespoons French dressing
1½ tablespoons salad oil
1 *very* soft boiled egg
3 teaspoon lemon juice
1 teaspoon sugar
1 teaspoon Worcester sauce
Garlic salt

Combine the ingredients and with a rotary beat well. Store in the refrigerator.

5. Savoury Lettuce Dressing

4 tablespoons olive oil
1½ tablespoons gin
Garlic salt
½ tablespoon fine chopped onion
2½ teaspoons lemon juice
½ teaspoon sugar
½ teaspoon dry mustard
Dash of tobasco

Combine the ingredients and shake very well. Store in the refrigerator.

6. Tangy Dressing

½ cup salad oil
½ teaspoon Worcester sauce
Garlic salt and pepper
3 tablespoons vinegar
1 tablespoon horseradish

Place all the ingredients in a glass jar. Close it well and shake till the mixture is very well blended. Store in the refrigerator.

Schmaltz is a delicious spread on bread. A spoonful mixed with mashed potato gives a rich flavour. It enhances soup and also baked dishes.

2 cups olive oil
2 thin sliced onions
Salt

Heat the oil to boiling and add the onion. Reduce the heat to slow simmering, hardly cooking. Simmer for $\frac{1}{2}$ hour or more till the onion becomes golden brown. Add the salt and pour through a strainer. Place the liquid in a jar and keep in the refrigerator to use when wanted.

SALADS

1. Asparagus and Egg Salad

1 tin drained asparagus
2–3 hard egg wedges
¼ cup salad oil
¼ cup olives
1½ tablespoons vinegar
1 tablespoon chopped pickles
½ tablespoon parsley
Cayenne
Salt

Place the asparagus on a serving dish. Beat the oil and vinegar creamy and add the pickles, parsley, cayenne, salt and pour this over the asparagus. Decorate with the egg wedges and olives.
(*3-4 people*)

2. Asparagus and Green Onion Salad

1 tin asparagus pieces
¼ cup chopped green onions
2 tablespoons mayonnaise
½ tablespoon top milk
1 tablespoons lemon juice
1 teaspoon sugar
½ teaspoon dry mustard
Salt

Place the drained asparagus on a serving dish and sprinkle it with half of the lemon juice. Combine the rest of the lemon juice, the mayonnaise, top milk, mustard, sugar, salt and spoon it over the asparagus. Sprinkle this with the green onion.
(*3-4 people*)

3. Avocado Salad

1½ cups avocado pieces
2–3 tablespoons yoghurt
1 tablespoon chopped onion
1 desertsspoon lemon juice
½ teaspoon sugar
½ teaspoon Worcester sauce
Salt

Combine and toss together the ingredients. Serve the salad with potato chips.

4. Avocado and Tomato Salad

1 medium peeled avocado
1 medium skinned sliced tomato
2–3 quartered hard eggs
Lettuce leaves
Ground almond sauce
Salt
Sugar

Halve the avocado lengthwise and then cut the halves across to get horseshoe shaped pieces; in turn halve these and to them add the tomato, sprinkled sugar and salt and the egg pieces. Line a salad bowl with lettuce and on it place the salad mixture. Over it pour the almond sauce.

Almond Sauce:
1 cup blanched pounded almonds
¼ cup salad oil
1 tablespoon lemon juice
1 teaspoon sugar
Garlic salt

Combine the almonds, lemon juice, sugar, garlic salt and pound it to a creamy paste. Drop by drop add the oil, beating constantly till the colour of the mixture becomes pale beige.

5. BANANA SALAD

4 ripe peeled bananas
$\frac{1}{4}$ cup mayonnaise
1 tablespoon top milk
Lettuce leaves
1 dessertspoon lemon juice
1 tablespoon chopped nuts
1 teaspoon sugar
Apricot jam

Halve the bananas lengthwise and at once dip them into the lemon juice to preserve their colour. Sandwich the halves together with apricot jam and arrange them on the lettuce lining a bowl. Combine the mayonnaise, top milk, sugar and pour the mixture over the bananas. Sprinkle with the nuts.
(*3–4 people*)

6. BEETROOT AND CREAM CHEESE SALAD

4 cooked beets
Mayonnaise
Lettuce leaves
$\frac{1}{2}$–$\frac{3}{4}$ cups cream cheese
$\frac{1}{4}$ cup chopped nuts
Seasoning

Hollow out the beets. Chop the scooped out parts and to this add the cream cheese, nuts, seasoning. Fill the beet hollows with the mixture. Place them on lettuce leaves and decorate them with a large blob of mayonnaise.
(*3–4 people*)

7. Beetroot Salad

4–5 cooked, peeled, sliced beets
2 tablespoons margarine
Paprika
Seasoning
1½ teaspoons made mustard
¾ teaspoon Worcester sauce
¾ teaspoon honey

In a saucepan heat the margarine, mustard, honey, Worcester sauce, seasoning to almost boiling point. Remove the pan from the fire and let the contents cool. Then pour the sauce over the beets and sprinkle with paprika.
(*3–4 people*)

8. Bread and Egg Salad

4–5 trimmed diced slices of bread
3–4 chopped hard eggs
1 cup shredded lettuce
French dressing
3 tablespoons melted margarine
1½ teaspoons garlic salt

Combine the margarine and garlic salt. Into this dip each piece of diced bread. Add the chopped eggs and add the French dressing. Toss well and place the mixture on the lettuce.
(*3–4 people*)

9. Cabbage and Apple Salad

½ tart peeled, chopped apple
½ chopped onion
2 cups shredded cabbage
½ cup Ideal or top milk
2 hard eggs
1 tablespoon lemon juice *or* vinegar
1 tablespoon melted margarine
1 teaspoon sugar
1 teaspoon dry mustard
Parsley sprigs
Salt

Combine the cabbage, onion, apple and toss. Blend together the sieved egg yolks, mustard, sugar, salt, margarine. Add the Ideal milk and mix well. Pour this over the cabbage mixture along with the lemon juice. Toss lightly and place in a bowl. Sprinkle with chopped egg whites and decorate with the parsley.
(*3-4 people*)

10. Cheese and Apple Salad

1 cup peeled cooked sliced potatoes
½ cup cubed cheese pieces
¼ cup shredded cabbage
2 tablespoons chopped pickles
Salad dressing
Salt

Combine all but the salad dressing. Add it to the mixture and toss lightly.

11. Cabbage and Cheese Salad

2 cups shredded cabbage
1 cup shredded spinach
½ cup grated cheese
½ cup chopped onion
¼ cup grated carrot
1 cup salad dressing
1 dessertspoon chopped parsley
Salt

Combine the cabbage, spinach, onion, parsley, salt and moisten and toss it with the salad dressing. Place the mixture in a bowl and garnish it with tiny balls made with combined carrot, cheese and a little salad dressing.
(*3-4 people*)

12. Cheese and Egg Loaf Salad

10 crushed cream crackers
1 cup grated cheese
Lettuce leaves
Salad dressing *or* mayonnaise
4–5 chopped hard eggs
7 chopped sweet pickles
Garlic salt

Combine all the ingredients but the lettuce with enough mayonnaise for a firm mixture. Press it into a greased loaf tin and chill for at least 1 hour. Cut the loaf into slices and arrange them on the lettuce.
(*3-4 people*)

13. Cabbage with Sauce Salad

2 cups shredded cabbage
¼ plus cups top milk
¼ cup vinegar
2 beaten eggs
1 tablespoon margarine
1 dessertspoon castor sugar
1 teaspoon dry mustard
Salt

In the top of a double boiler heat the vinegar, and then remove the pan from the heat. Combine the sugar, mustard, salt, beaten eggs and to this add very gradually the warm vinegar, stirring. Return it to the heat and stir constantly till it thickens. Again remove it from the heat and slowly add the top milk, stirring. While still warm pour the sauce over the cabbage and toss.

14. Cooked Spinach Salad

2 cups cooked chopped spinach
1 cup grated cheese
2 beaten eggs
Top milk
1 thick trimmed slice of crumbled bread
Margarine
Lettuce leaves
Small pickled onions
Sliced radishes
Salt

Squeeze the spinach dry and add the bread crumbs, cheese, eggs, salt and enough top milk for a slack mixture. Place it in a greased square oven tin. Dot with margarine and cover the tin. Bake for about 25 minutes and then bake uncovered for 5 minutes in a 400°F. oven. Remove the tin from the oven and let cool. Then cut into squares and place them on the lettuce. Decorate with the small onions and sliced radishes.
(*3–4 people*)

15. Cucumber Salad

1½ cups coarsely chopped cucumbers clear of the white parts
½ cup walnut halves
½ cup salad cream *or* mayonnaise
Lettuce leaves
Paprika
Salt

Combine the cucumber, mayonnaise, paprika, salt and toss. Place this on the lettuce leaves and decorate with the walnut halves.

16. Dried Bean and Pickle Salad

1 cup overnight soaked, cooked dried beans
½ cup chopped sweet pickles
2 sliced hard eggs
Lettuce leaves
1 tablespoon chopped celery *or* chives
1 tablespoon mayonnaise
1 tablespoon top milk
Salt

Drain the beans and add the pickles, celery, combined mayonnaise and top milk, salt. Toss the mixture and place it in a lettuce lined bowl. Decorate with the egg slices.

17. Egg and Mint Salad

1 large cup yoghurt
¼ cup chopped mint
¼ cup vinegar
4 hard eggs
Lettuce leaves
2 teaspoons vinegar
2 teaspoons sugar
1 teaspoon made mustard
Salt

Mash 1 hard egg yolk and add the mustard, sugar, salt. Gradually add the vinegar and the yoghurt. Toss lightly and then add the three remaining thick sliced hard eggs. Then add the combined chopped remaining hard white egg and the mint and again toss lightly. Place on the lettuce leaves.

18. GREEN BEAN SALAD

$1\frac{1}{2}$ cups cooked green beans
$\frac{3}{4}$ cup warm milk
1 tablespoon lemon juice
$\frac{3}{4}$ tablespoon flour and 1 of margarine
1 beaten egg yolk
$\frac{1}{2}$ teaspoon dry mustard
$\frac{1}{2}$ teaspoon sugar
Salt

In the top of a double boiler place the margarine, flour, mustard, salt. Mix them and then add the egg yolk, blending it in. Gradually add the milk and cook, stirring till thickened. Remove the pan from the heat and add the sugar and lemon juice, stirring. Place the beans in a bowl and pour the sauce over.

19. GREEN BEANS WITH PICKLES

$1\frac{1}{2}$ cups cooked green beans
$\frac{3}{4}$ cups stock
1 teaspoon Worcester sauce *or* marmite
$\frac{1}{2}$ teaspoon sugar
1 tablespoon flour
$\frac{1}{2}$ tablespoon vinegar
1 tablespoon chopped pickles
Salt

In the top of a double boiler place the flour, sugar, salt, vinegar, Worcester sauce, mixing. Gradually add the stock and stir till thickened. Add the pickles and heat them. Remove the pan from the fire and let the mixture cool. Then pour it over the green beans.

20. HARD EGG SALAD

5 hard eggs halved lengthwise
1½ cups shredded lettuce
½ cup mayonnaise
Tobasco sauce
Lettuce leaves
1 tablespoon top milk
1 tablespoon chopped green olives
1 tablespoon chopped green onions
2 teaspoons chopped parsley
1 teaspoon lemon juice
Salt

Spread out the lettuce on a platter and on it arrange the halved hard eggs, face down. Cover them with a sauce made by mixing the rest of the ingredients.

21. HARICOT SALAD

1 tin drained haricots
½ cup salad dressing
2 teaspoons chopped parsley
½ teaspoon sugar
1 tablespoon sliced green olives
1½ tablespoons black olives
Garlic salt

Combine all but the black olives and place the mixture in a bowl. Garnish it with the black olives.

1½ cups peeled sliced warm potatoes
1 tablespoon salad oil
2 tablespoons chopped onion
1 tablespoons green pepper
1 teaspoon wine vinegar
½ teaspoon honey
¼ teaspoon lemon juice
¼ teaspoon lemon rind
¼ teaspoon thyme
Garlic salt

Pound the lemon rind, thyme, salt and add the combined honey, lemon juice and vinegar. Gradually add the salad oil, mixing, and pour the sauce over the potatoes. Then fry the onion and green pepper and add it to the salad. Toss gently till well mixed. Keep warm if wished or use cold.

23. LETTUCE TOSS

1½ cups shredded lettuce
¼ cup chopped chives
¼ cup mayonnaise
Salt
1 teaspoon vinegar
1 teaspoon sugar
1 teaspoon made mustard
1 teaspoon horseradish

Toss the lettuce and chives together and pour over the combined mayonnaise, vinegar, sugar, mustard, horseradish, salt.

24. MACARONI SALAD

$\frac{1}{2}$ cup cooked and cut macaroni pieces *or* use noodles
$\frac{1}{4}$ cup cooked green peas
$\frac{1}{4}$ cup cooked diced carrots
$\frac{1}{4}$ cup asparagus tips (optional)
Mayonnaise
Seasoning

Combine the ingredients and toss them.
(*3- 4 people*)

25. NEW POTATO SALAD

12 cooked skinned new potatoes
$\frac{1}{2}$ cup small cheese cubes
$\frac{1}{4}$ cup French dressing
Lettuce leaves
2 dill pickles sliced diagonally
$\frac{1}{2}$ teaspoon fennel or other herb
Salt

Toss together the potatoes, dill, cheese cubes, French dressing, salt and place the mixture on a lettuce lined bowl. Sprinkle with the fennel.
(*3 4 people*)

26. ONION SALAD

6–7 medium boiled onions
2 beaten eggs
1 cup vinegar
1 dessertspoon sugar
Salt

In the top of a double boiler place the vinegar and sugar and stir till the sugar melts. Add the eggs and with a rotary beat the mixture till it thickens. Pour the sauce over the onions.

(*3 4 people*)

27. POTATO CURRY SALAD

1½ cups cooked potato pieces
1 tablespoon yoghurt or sour cream
1 tablespoon mayonnaise
1½ tablespoons chopped onion
1½ tablespoons sliced stuffed olives
1 teaspoon curry powder
½ teaspoon lemon juice
¼ teaspoon celery seed
¼ teaspoon sugar
2 hard eggs
Salt

Toss together the potato, celery seed, salt. Over this pour the combined yoghurt, mayonnaise, onion, 1 mashed egg yolk, curry powder, lemon juice, sugar and toss again. Decorate with the sieved remaining yolk and the chopped egg whites, on top of which arrange the sliced olives.

28. POTATO AND HARD EGG SALAD

5 medium cooked, skinned potatoes
1 large chopped onion
3 hard eggs
¼ plus cup mayonnaise
Cayenne
Salt

Cut the potatoes into neat cubes and add the onion and mayonnaise, tossing gently. Add the cayenne and salt and fold in 2

chopped hard eggs. Slice the other hard egg and arrange it on the salad.
(*3–4 people*)

29. POTATO SALAD WITH SAUCE

1½ cups skinned cooked sliced potatoes
1 cup potato water *or* milk
1 small chopped onion
1 teaspoons sugar
2 teaspoons chopped parsley
1 tablespoon vinegar
¾ tablespoon flour
1 teaspoon made mustard
Seasoning

Bring the stock to the boil and add a paste made with potato water, flour, mustard, seasoning, stirring till thickened. Combine the potato, onion, parsley and add the combined vinegar and sugar, tossing. Pour the sauce over.

30. RICE AND GREEN PEA SALAD

1½ cups cooked rice
½ cup grated cheese
½ cup thin mayonnaise
¼ tin drained green peas
3 chopped hard eggs
1 tablespoon chopped parsley
Seasoning

Combine all but the parsley which then sprinkle on top.
(*3- 4 people*)

31. Rice Salad

1½ cups cooked rice
¼ cup thinned mayonnaise
¼ cup grated raw carrot
5–6 chopped spring onions
2 sliced gherkins
2 sliced hard eggs
Seasoning

Combine and toss all but the hard egg. Then arrange the hard egg slices on top.

32. Scrambled Egg Salad

1½ cups peeled cooked cubed potatoes
1 large firm skinned chopped tomato
1 chopped onion
1 tablespoon margarine
4–5 eggs
Lettuce leaves
1 tablespoon chopped parsley
1 teaspoon chopped mint
1 teaspoon thyme
Salad dressing
Salt

With the herbs and salt scramble the eggs lightly. Let them cool and then add them to the potato, tomato, onion. Pour over some salad dressing and toss the mixture. Place it on the salad leaves. (*3–4 people*)

33. Spinach and Potato Salad

1 cup peeled cooked cubed potatoes
1 cup raw fine chopped young spinach
¼ cup chopped onion *or* chives
3 sliced hard eggs
1 tablespoon chopped parsley
4–5 tablespoons salad dressing
Salt

Combine all but the eggs and toss lightly. Garnish with the eggs.

34. Spinach Salad

1½ cups cooked chopped spinach
½ cup breadcrumbs
½ cup grated cheese
¼ cup top milk
1 tablespoon margarine
2–3 beaten eggs
Seasoning
Lettuce leaves

Squeeze the spinach dry and add the crumbs, cheese, seasoning and the combined eggs and top milk. Place the mixture in a greased oven pan and cover it. Bake 25 minutes in a 400°F. oven. Remove it from the heat and let it cool. Then cut the slab into squares and serve them on lettuce.
(*3–4 peopie*)

35. TOMATO AND AVOCADO SALAD

1 skinned and stoned avocado
2 large firm skinned sliced tomatoes
$1\frac{1}{2}$ cups shredded lettuce
A little lemon juice or vinegar
$\frac{1}{2}$ chopped onion
3–4 tablespoons mayonnaise
Sugar
Salt
Paprika

On a platter spread out the lettuce. Cover it with the tomato slices and sprinkle them with sugar, salt and the onion. Cut the avocado into neat even lengths and arrange them on the tomato in the shape of a flower, leaving the centre open for space to place the mayonnaise like a disc. Sprinkle with paprika.
(*3- 4 people*)

36. TOMATO AND CREAM CHEESE SALAD

4 large firm tomatoes
$\frac{3}{4}$–1 cup cream cheese
Lettuce leaves
Mayonnaise
Sugar
Salt

From their tops cut the tomatoes right around them for $\frac{1}{2}$ of the way down, and see to it that there will be an *uneven* number of wedges. Remove alternate wedges and sprinkle the open places with sugar and salt. Now fill the gaps where the wedges were with cream cheese, rounding them off neatly. Place the tomatoes on the lettuce and give each of them a good blob of mayonnaise on top.
(*3 4 people*)

VEGETABLES

1. ASPARAGUS PANCAKES

Pancakes
Tinned drained asparagus
Enriched white sauce, *or* cheese
or any other desired sauce

Around each asparagus length roll a pancake. Place them on an oven serving dish and pour the sauce over. Warm this before serving.

2. ASPARAGUS TART

Pastry lined piedish
1 small tin drained asparagus pieces
1 small tin asparagus soup
3 quartered hard eggs
1 raw egg beaten
$\frac{1}{4}$ cup grated cheese
Cayenne
Salt

Spread the asparagus pieces on the base of the pastry and arrange the hard egg pieces over them. Pour over the combined egg, soup and seasoning. Sprinkle with the cheese and bake till set in a 325–350°F. oven.
(*3 4 people*)

3. CHEESE ASPARAGUS

1 tin drained asparagus lengths
¼ cup onion butter
½ cup cheese diced small
1½ tablespoons Parmesan cheese flakes
Seasoning

Arrange the asparagus on a square oven dish and cover it with grated onion butter. Sprinkle with the combined 2 cheeses and bake for 10 minutes till melted and golden.

Onion Butter:
1 envelope onion soup
½ cup grated margarine *or* butter
Seasoning

Combine the ingredients and chill them well before grating this over the asparagus.

4. POTATO ASPARAGUS

1 tin drained asparagus lengths
1½ cups soft enriched mashed potato
1 teaspoon lemon juice
Margarine
½ teaspoon dry sage
Seasoning

Arrange the asparagus in a square oven dish and sprinkle it with the lemon juice, sage, seasoning. Dot with margarine and cover with a layer of the mashed potato. Bake golden in a 375°F. oven. (*3–4 people*)

5. BEETROOT CAKES

1 large cooked peeled mashed beetroot
1 cup breadcrumbs and extra crumbs
1 cup milk
2 beaten eggs
Margarine
Seasoning

Soak the breadcrumbs in the milk for 10 minutes and then add the beetroot, eggs, seasoning and mix well. Shape small cakes and dip them all over in the extra crumbs. Fry them golden.

6. BAKED BEETROOT

Beetroots baked in the oven are of a deeper colour and stronger flavour than those boiled in water. To bake them wash well, wrap each one in greased paper or foil and bake as for baked potatoes. They will take about the same time to cook as baked potatoes. Peel them when they are done.

7. BEETROOT LEAVES SALAD

2 cups green beetroot leaves
$\frac{3}{4}$ cup water
$\frac{1}{2}$ cup salad dressing
2–3 sliced hard eggs
Worcester sauce
Seasoning

Remove the stalks from the beetroot leaves and then boil the leaves for about 20 minutes in the water. Then press them dry on a sieve, place them in a bowl and add the Worcester sauce and seasoning, tossing well. Place this in a mould and press it firmly in. Let it cool and then turn it out on to a serving dish. Pour the dressing over and decorate with the egg slices.
(*3–4 people*)

8. BEETROOT SALAD

4–5 cooked peeled beets
1 medium sliced onion
1 tablespoon maizena
3 cloves
2 teaspoons vinegar
1 teaspoon sugar
2 teaspoons margarine
Salt

Cut the beets into thickish slices and in a saucepan cover them with water. Add the onion, cloves, salt and cook for half an hour. Make a paste of maizena and water and add it to the mixture, stirring till thickened. Then remove the pan from the fire and add the margarine, vinegar and sugar. Let it cool and place it in a serving bowl.
(*3–4 people*)

9. BAKED BRINJAL

1 medium peeled brinjal
3 tablespoons melted margarine
Breadcrumbs
Seasoning

Cut the brinjal into $\frac{1}{3}$ inch thick rounds. Dip them into the melted margarine and then into the crumbs. Place them on a greased oven sheet. Sprinkle them with seasoning and bake for about 20 minutes in a hottish oven.

10. CUSTARD BRINJAL

1 medium peeled sliced brinjal
½ cup milk
¼ cup top milk
½–¾ cup tomato sauce
1 beaten egg
2 tablespoons oil
4 tablespoons grated cheese
2 tablespoons fresh crumbs
Salt
Flour

Sprinkle the brinjal slices with salt and let them sweat for 15–20 minutes. Dry them and sprinkle them with flour. Fry them golden and drain them. Place them in an oven dish and pour over the combined milk, top milk, egg and a dash of salt. Bake this for 30–40 minutes in a 325°F. oven and remove the dish from the oven. Now over the custard pour the tomato sauce. Sprinkle with the combined cheese and crumbs and grill golden. N.B. Leeks may be used instead of brinjals. Cut 2 inch lengths and boil them tender for 5 minutes. Drain and place them in an oven dish and then proceed as above for brinjals slices.
(*3–4 people*)

11. BRINJAL OMELETTE

1 small peeled brinjal
Omelette mixture
Oil
Salt

Slice the brinjal and soak the slices for half an hour in salt water. Drain and cut the slices into small cubes. Fry them golden and again drain them. Add them to the omelette mixture and then fry the omelette, fold it and serve with chips.

Omelette Mixture:
3 beaten eggs
¼ cup milk
1 tablespoon top milk
½ teaspoon baking powder
Margarine
Seasoning

Combine the ingredients and add the brinjal cubes. During the frying lift the sides of the omelette to let the surplus liquid run below.

12. BOILED CABBAGE

1 small cabbage
1 cup milk
1 tablespoon flour
Nutmeg
Salt

Cut the inner leaves of the cabbage into large pieces and half cook them in boiling water, keeping the lid of the pan on. Drain and chop the cabbage. Sprinkle it with the flour and return it to a clean pan. Add the milk and after bringing it to the boil, simmer the mixture gently for 10 minutes and place it in a serving dish. Sprinkle it with the nutmeg.
(3–4 people)

13. CABBAGE PANCAKES

1 cup finely chopped cabbage
1½ cups pancake batter
1 tablespoon grated onion
Margarine or oil
Seasoning

Combine the cabbage, onion, seasoning, batter and fry pancakes a bit thicker than usual. Serve with a savoury sauce.

14. Cabbage Curry

2 cups shredded cabbage
1 cup salted water
1 dessertspoon chutney
1 tablespoon flour
1 tablespoon margarine
2 teaspoon curry powder
Salt

Melt the margarine and add the curry powder, blending. Add the cabbage and fry for 5 minutes. Then add the salted water and cook till tender. Thicken with a paste of flour and a little water, stirring well.

15. Carrot Croquettes

2 cups cooked mashed carrots
2 tablespoons flour
2 tablespoons margarine
1 cup milk
Fried onions
3 eggs
Oil
Breadcrumbs
Seasoning

Blend melted margarine and the flour and remove the pan from the fire. Gradually add the milk, stirring well. Add the combined carrots, 2 beaten eggs, seasoning and mix. Let the mixture cool and then shape croquettes. Dip them into 1 beaten egg and then into crumbs. Fry in deep hot oil till golden. When serving place each croquette with a spoon of fried onion and serve with mashed potato.

16. Cheese Carrots

1 cup cooked sliced carrots
1 cup grated cheese
Cayenne and salt

Place a layer of the drained carrots in a greased oven dish. Sprinkle them with cayenne and salt and cover them with a thick layer of grated cheese. Bake about 10 minutes till the cheese melts.

17. Carrots with Macaroni or Spaghetti

1½ cups thin sliced carrots
1 cup cooked macaroni pieces
¾ cup grated cheese
Fried tomato halves
Margarine
Seasoning

Fry the carrot slices in enough margarine for about 10 minutes, tossing. Add the seasoning and mix them with the macaroni, distributing them evenly. Place this in a warm serving dish and sprinkle the mixture with cheese. Surround it with the fried tomatoes.
(*3–4 people*)

18. Carrot and Potato Heaps

1 cup sliced carrots
1 cup sliced potatoes
2 tablespoons hot milk
1 tablespoons margarine
Seasoning

Cook the carrot slices in water for 10 minutes and then add the potato slices. Cook till they are tender and then drain and mash them. Add the seasoning and margarine and mix and add the hot milk, beating smooth. Place small heaps of the mixture on a greased oven sheet and bake until they become golden.

19. YOUNG CARROTS

12–15 scraped uncut young carrots
Carrot water
1 tablespoon flour
1 tablespoon margarine
$\frac{1}{2}$ tablespoon chopped parsley
Salt

In water cook the carrots 8–10 minutes. Drain them and keep the carrot water. Make a sauce by blending melted margarine and the flour and gradually adding to it the carrot water, stirring till thickened. Return the carrots to the saucepan and simmer for 5 minutes. Sprinkle with *or* add the parsley to the mixture.
(*3–4 people*)

20. CAULIFLOWER WITH MUSTARD PICKLES

1 small cooked cauliflower
1 cup white sauce
$1\frac{1}{2}$ tablespoons chopped mustard pickles
Salt

Place the cauliflower in a warm serving dish and pour over it the combined white sauce, mustard pickles and salt.
(*3–4 people*)

21. Savoury Cauliflower

1 small cooked drained cauliflower
½ cup chopped fried chives
1 teaspoon sugar
1 tablespoon olive oil
½ tablespoon vinegar
Cayenne
Salt

In a greased oven dish place the cauliflower. Sprinkle it with the combined oil, chives, vinegar, sugar, salt. Place the dish in a slow oven and bake for 10 minutes.
(*3–4 people*)

22. Cauliflower Sprigs with Eggs

1½ cups partly cooked drained cauliflower sprigs
¼ cup chopped fried onion
2–3 beaten eggs
1 tablespoon margarine
½ teaspoon caraway seeds
Salt

In a greased oven dish place the combined cauliflower sprigs, fried onion, caraway seeds. Pour over it the combined eggs and seasoning and bake for a few minutes. Serve with mashed potatoes.

23. Fried Cauliflower Florets

1 half boiled small cauliflower
1 cup batter
1 cup breadcrumbs
1 tablespoon flour
Oil
Seasoning

Divide the cauliflower into florets and dust them with combined flour and seasoning. Dip them well into the batter and then into the crumbs. Fry golden in hot oil. Serve with mashed potatoes.
(*3–4 people*)

24. Green Beans with White Sauce

2 cups cooked green beans
1 cup warm milk
1 beaten egg
Seasoning
1 tablespoon cream *or* top milk
1 tablespoon flour
1 tablespoon melted margarine

Over heat blend the margarine and flour. Gradually add the combined milk and cream, stirring till smooth. Remove the pan from the heat and let the mixture cool a little and add the beaten egg, mixing well. Add the seasoning and then the beans and reheat.
(*3–4 people*)

25. Green Beans with Mustard Sauce

2 cups cooked green beans
1 cup warm milk
1 eggyolk
2 teaspoons vinegar
1 teaspoon sugar
1 teaspoon made mustard
Salt

Combine the beaten yolk, mustard, sugar, salt and gradually add the hot milk, stirring till thickened. Add the vinegar and bring the sauce to the boil. Pour it over the beans. The sauce will look curdled.
(*3–4 people*)

26. Green Beans with Tomato

2 cups cooked green beans
¼ cup chopped green onion tops
1 skinned chopped tomato
¼ cup oil
½ tablespoon chopped parsley
1 teaspoon sugar
Salt

Fry the onion for 5 minutes and add the tomato and parsley. Simmer for 5 minutes and add the beans. Add the sugar and salt and simmer again till well heated.
(*3–4 people*)

27. Herb Green Beans

2 cups cooked green beans
½ cup chopped onion
¼ cup margarine
Seasoning and Paprika
2 tablespoons chopped parsley
½ tablespoon lemon juice
½ teaspoon thyme
½ teaspoon sugar

Fry the onion soft and add all the rest of the ingredients but the beans. Simmer a few minutes and pour the sauce over the beans.
(*3–4 people*)

28. Haricot Snow

1½ cups haricots soaked overnight
3 tablespoons top milk *or* cream
3 tablespoons margarine
1 egg
1 dessertspoon chopped parsley
Seasoning

Cook the beans tender and sieve them. In a pan melt the margarine and add the beans, top milk, beaten eggyolk, seasoning, and gently cook for 5 minutes, stirring. Remove the pan from the fire and let the mixture cool a little. Fold in the stiff eggwhites and sprinkle with parsley. Warm carefully before serving.

29. STEWED LEEKS

1½ cups 1½ inch long leek pieces
½ cup leek water
¼ cup vinegar
1 beaten egg
1 dessertspoon flour
1 dessertspoon margarine
1½ teaspoons sugar
Salt

Boil the leek pieces tender. Drain them and keep the leek water. Make a sauce with melted margarine, blended in flour and gradually added leek water. Add the cooked leeks and salt and simmer the mixture for 5–10 minutes. Let it cool a bit and add the egg, mixing well. Reheat the mixture gently.

30. LEEK RICE

1½ cups quartered leeks
¾ cup skinned sliced tomatoes
½ cup rice
2 tablespoons margarine
Seasoning
2 teaspoons sugar

Melt the margarine and fry the leek pieces 5 minutes. Add the rice and fry 3 minutes, stirring. Add the tomato, sugar, seasoning, mixing and cover the mixture with water. Cook about half an hour till the liquid is absorbed. Can be eaten hot or cold.
(*3–4 people*)

31. LENTILS

1 cup lentils soaked overnight
1 small sliced onion
1 dessertspoon margarine
1 teaspoon tumeric
1 bayleaf
Seasoning

Cook the lentils soft and sieve them. Fry the onion and add it to them. Add the tumeric, bayleaf, seasoning and cover with cold water. Cook, stirring, till thickened. Serve with fried tomatoes.

32. STUFFED MARROWS

1 long lengthwise halved marrow
Stuffing
Vegetable stock

With a spoon scrape the seeds from the marrow halves. Fill the hollows with stuffing and place them on a greased oven dish. Around them pour a little stock *or* marmite water. With it paste the marrow halves now and again while they are cooking. Serve with a salad.

Stuffing:
1¼ cups bread cubes
½ cup melted margarine
¼ cup stock
½ cup chopped onion
½ teaspoon thyme
¼ teaspoon sage
Salt
Paprika

Combine the ingredients.

33. TOMATO MUSHROOMS

1½ cups thick sliced mushrooms
½ cup tomato puree
2 tablespoons oil
1 teaspoon chopped mint
Garlic salt

Heat the oil well and add the mushrooms, mint and garlic salt. Cook for 5 minutes and add the tomato puree. Simmer for 10 minutes and serve with enriched mashed potatoes.

34. MUSHROOMS WITH YOGHURT

1½ cups sliced mushrooms
1 small chopped onion
½ cup yoghurt
1½ tablespoons margarine
1 dessertspoon flour
Seasoning

In the margarine fry the onion for 3 minutes. Add the mushrooms and fry again for about 10 minutes till tender. Combine the flour, yoghurt, seasoning and add this to the mixture. Simmer for 5 minutes and serve with enriched rice.

35. MUSHROOM TOAST

4 medium mushrooms
4 toast slices buttered
¾ cup grated cheese
¼ cup margarine
1½ cups water
1 dessertspoon maizena
Seasoning

Fry the mushrooms, their stems removed, for about 10 minutes till tender. Drain and then place them on the toast. Boil the stems for 10–15 minutes in the water and then remove them. To the hot liquid add a paste of maizena and a little water. Cook, stirring till thickened. Add seasoning to taste and pour the sauce over the mushrooms. Sprinkle thickly with cheese and bake till golden in a hottish oven.

36. Onion and Potato Cake

2 cups enriched mashed potato
$\frac{1}{4}$ cup melted margarine
2 large sliced onions
Seasoning

In part of the margarine fry the onions deep golden. Mix them with the potato and spread a $\frac{3}{4}$ inch thick layer of this on a greased oven dish. Sprinkle with the rest of the margarine and bake golden in a 400°F· oven.

37. Devilled Onions

6 cooked chopped onions
$1\frac{1}{2}$ cups white sauce
$\frac{1}{2}$ cup grated cheese
$\frac{1}{4}$ cup breadcrumbs
2 chopped hard eggs
1 teaspoon made mustard
Cayenne
Salt

Combine all the ingredients but the cheese and crumbs. Place the mixture in an oven dish and sprinkle it with the combined cheese and crumbs. Bake golden.
(*3–4 people*)

38. Savoury Parsnips

2 cups sliced parsnips
¼ cup melted margarine
1 dessertspoon flour
1 teaspoon brown sugar
1 teaspoon dry mustard
Cayenne
Salt

Cook the parsnips tender in salted water. Drain and then place them in a greased oven dish. Sprinkle with combined flour, sugar, mustard and then with cayenne. Pour the margarine over. Bake 15–20 minutes in a medium oven.
(*3–4 people*)

39. Potato Crisps

2 large peeled halved lengthwise potatoes
Oil
Salt

Using a potato peeler, cut very thin slices from the halved potatoes. In deep hot oil cook them crisp and golden. Drain them on brown paper and sprinkle them with salt. Dry them on fresh brown paper. They will stay crisp if not placed in a covered container. If wanted warm, they can be heated in a very slow oven.

40. Raw Potato Cakes

2 cups grated raw potato
3 tablespoons milk
2 tablespoons flour
1 medium chopped onion
1 teaspoon baking powder
¼ teaspoon marjoram
Garlic salt

Drain the potato and add the rest of the ingredients, mixing well. Place a thickish layer in a flat greased oven dish and bake for about half an hour *or* shape cakes and fry in hot oil.

41. SPECIAL MASHED POTATOES

The warm contents of 4 large baked potatoes
2–3 tablespoons top milk
1½ tablespoons margarine
2 eggs
Nutmeg
Seasoning

For 3 minutes cook the combined mashed contents of the potatoes, top milk, beaten egg yolks, seasoning and remove the mixture from the fire. Fold in the stiffly beaten egg whites and with 2 greased tablespoons scoop out meringue-like shapes. Place them on a greased oven sheet and bake golden. Delicious with nut dishes.
(*3–4 people*)

42. NEW POTATOES

10–15 tiny new potatoes in their skins
¼–½ cup melted margarine
1 tablespoon sour cream or mild vinegar
Seasoning
1 tablespoon chopped dill pickles
or parsley

If the skins of the new potatoes are very thin keep them on. Add the rest of the ingredients and keep warm.
(*3–4 people*)

43. Yoghurt Potatoes

1½ cups peeled diced potatoes
¼ cup yoghurt
1 tablespoon flour
1 dessertspoon chopped onion
1 dessertspoon margarine
2 teaspoons chopped parsley
½ teaspoon thyme
1 bayleaf
Seasoning

Cook the diced potatoes in a little water and strain them but keep the potato water. Fry the onion golden and add the flour, mixing. Gradually add the potato water, stirring till thickened. Add the potato, thyme, bayleaf and seasoning and simmer 5 minutes. Remove the bayleaf and let the mixture cool. Add the yoghurt and toss well. When serving sprinkle with parsley. Can be used as a salad.

44. Baked Spinach Pancakes

1½ cups batter
1 cup cooked, chopped seasoned spinach
1¼ cup milk
2 beaten eggs
Margarine
Salt

Fry small thin pancakes with the batter. On each place a little of the spinach puree. Roll up the pancakes and place them side by side in a greased oven dish. Combine the eggs, milk and salt and pour the custard over the pancakes. Bake till the custard sets.

Batter:
2 beaten eggs
1¼ cups milk
Enough flour for a thin batter
Salt

Combine the ingredients and beat till smooth.
(*4–5 people*)

45. SPINACH PUREE

2 cups spinach
1 medium chopped onion
½ teaspoon mace
1½ tablespoons flour
1 tablespoon margarine
4 tablespoons cold water
Garlic salt
Pepper

In a covered pan cook the spinach for 5 minutes without water. Then chop it finely. Fry the onion and add it. Sprinkle this with the flour and cook for 1 minute, stirring. Gradually add the cold water, blending well. Now add the spinach and the rest of the ingredients and simmer for 5 minutes. If the puree is too thick add a little water or stock.

46. DELICIOUS SPINACH

1½ cups cooked chopped spinach
¼ cup cream or top milk
1 sliced hard egg
1½ tablespoons horseradish
1½ tablespoons soft margarine
Seasoning

Combine all but the egg and heat gently. Garnish with the egg slices.

47. SPINACH FRITTERS

1½ cups dry cooked chopped spinach
2–3 beaten eggs
½ cup breadcrumbs
1½ tablespoons melted margarine
Oil
Seasoning

Combine all the ingredients but the oil. With floured hands shape neat cakes or balls. Fry golden and drain.

48. SPINACH ROLL

1½ cups thick soft creamy spinach puree
1¼ cups milk
½ cup grated cheese
2 teaspoons baking powder
2½ tablespoons flour
2 tablespoons margarine
3 beaten eggs
Seasoning

Combine all the ingredients but the spinach and cheese and beat smooth. Pour the mixture into a greased, flat oblong pan and bake for 10–15 minutes till cooked but *not* browned. Turn this out on to a floured towel or paper and spread its surface with the spinach puree. Roll it up as for a jelly roll and before serving sprinkle it with the cheese.
(*3–4 people*)

49. TOMATO SPINACH

2 cups cooked chopped seasoned spinach
1 cup skinned cooked sieved tomatoes
$\frac{1}{4}$ cup salad dressing
3 chopped hard eggs
2 teaspoons sugar
Salt

In a greased oven dish place a 2 inch thick layer of spinach puree. Combine the tomato, salad dressing, sugar, salt and cover the spinach layer with it. Sprinkle with the chopped eggs and gently heat through in the oven.

51. SWEETCORN OYSTERS

$1\frac{1}{2}$ cups grated sweetcorn cobs
2 beaten eggs
$1\frac{1}{2}$ tablespoons flour
Oil or margarine
Seasoning

Combine all the ingredients but the oil. Heat the oil well and into it drop spoonfuls of the corn mixture. Fry them golden. Sweetcorn oysters may also be made by draining tinned sweetcorn and using it as above.

52. TOMATO PIE

Pastry lined piedish
$1\frac{1}{4}$ cups skinned tomato pulp
1 cup breadcrumbs
1 cup grated cheese
1 small chopped onion
1 tablespoon oil
Seasoning

Combine the tomato pulp, half the breadcrumbs, half the cheese, the onion and seasoning. Place the mixture on the pastry, spreading it out evenly. Combine the rest of the cheese and crumbs and sprinkle it over the filling. Then sprinkle the oil and bake about half an hour in a medium oven.

The Pastry:
1½ cups flour
Salt
2 tablespoons oil
3–4 tablespoons skim milk

Sift the flour and salt. All at once pour on it the combined oil and milk. With a fork mix till well dampened. To line the pie dish with it, press it in firmly and evenly. Prick the entire surface. If wished extra oil may be used to make a richer pastry.

52. CHINESE TURNIPS

4 peeled sliced turnips
½ cup chopped green onion sticks
1 teaspoon peanut butter
2 teaspoons oil
Seasoning

Cook the turnips tender in just enough water to half cover them. Drain and to them add the combined peanut butter and oil beaten smooth. Add the green onion and seasoning, tossing well.

53. POTATO TURNIPS

1¼ cups peeled sliced turnips
¾ cups peeled sliced potatoes
¼ cup stock or cream
1 dessertspoon margarine
Seasoning

In salted water simmer the turnips for about 15 minutes. Add the potato slices and cook till they are soft. Drain and mash the mixture. Add a little cream and beat and then the margarine and seasoning, beating smooth. Heat gently.
(*3–4 people*)

54. TURNIPS WITH MUSTARD

1½ cups peeled cubed turnips
¾ cup stock
¾ cup chopped onion
1½ tablespoons margarine
1 tablespoon flour
1½ teaspoons made mustard
Seasoning

Fry the turnips golden. Sprinkle them with flour, tossing, and gradually add the stock, stirring well. Add the onion, mustard, seasoning and simmer for about 20 minutes.
(*3–4 people*)

55. YOUNG TURNIPS

1½ cups peeled, sliced *or* diced young turnips
1½ tablespoons margarine
1½ tablespoons flour
¾ cup cold water
¾ cup hot water
1 teaspoon marmite *or* Worcester sauce
Pepper to taste

Scald the turnips with the hot water. Drain them and add a sauce made with melted margarine, added flour, gradually added cold water, marmite, pepper, and beat smooth. Simmer for about 10 minutes.

FISH

1. BAKED FISH

6 fish fillets *or* steaks
4 tablespoons oil
2 tablespoons lemon juice
2 teaspoons grated onion
Salt

Sprinkle the fish pieces with salt and dip them into the combined oil, lemon juice and onion. Place them on a greased flat oven dish and over them pour the remaining oil mixture in which they were dipped. Bake 20–30 minutes in a 375°F. oven till the fish flakes when tested with a fork.
(*3–4 people*)

2. BAKED FISH WITH CORN FLAKES

4–5 $\frac{1}{2}$ inch thick fish steaks
1$\frac{1}{2}$ cups half crushed corn flakes
$\frac{1}{2}$ cup milk
2 tablespoons melted butter *or* margarine
Salt

Dissolve the salt in the milk and dip the fish pieces in it. Then dip them all over in the flakes and place them on a greased oven sheet. Pour the melted butter over the fish and bake for 20–30 minutes in a 400°F. oven.
(*4 people*)

3. Broiled Fish

1 prepared small fish
1 cup milk
1 cup skinless seeded white grapes
1 tablespoon margarine
Seasoning
Paprika

Place the fish in a greased oven dish and dot it with margarine. Sprinkle with the seasoning and the paprika and add the grapes. Pour the milk around the fish. Bake for 20–30 minutes in a moderate oven.

4. Baked Fish with Cheese

4–5 fish slices
½ cup milk
¼ cup top milk
1 cup grated cheese
1 sliced onion
1 dessertspoon chopped parsley
1 tablespoon margarine
Seasoning

Place the onion on a greased oven dish. On it arrange the fish. Sprinkle it with seasoning, dot it with margarine and pour the milk around it. Cover the dish and bake the contents for 15 minutes. Then uncover the dish and add the top milk and combined cheese and parsley. Bake golden and serve with boiled potatoes.
(*3–4 people*)

5. Salt Cod with Haricots

4–5 pieces freshened salt cod
$\frac{3}{4}$ cup soaked and cooked haricots
$\frac{1}{4}$ cup liquid in which beans were cooked
1 chopped onion
1 dessertspoon salad oil
1 dessertspoon melted margarine
2 teaspoons chopped parsley
$\frac{1}{2}$ teaspoon mixed herbs
Garlic salt

Fry the onion golden in the combined oil and margarine. Add the bean liquid and also $\frac{1}{4}$ cup of sieved haricots, mixing. Add the garlic salt, mixed herbs and the whole haricots. Then add the fish pieces and simmer for 15–20 minutes. Sprinkle with parsley before serving and fried bread slices make a nice addition.

(*3–4 people*)

6. Baked Fish Fillets with Anchovies

4–5 fish fillets
6 mashed anchovies
$\frac{1}{2}$ cup breadcrumbs
3 tablespoons salad oil
2 tablespoons melted margarine
1 dessertspoon chopped parsley
Pepper

Place the fillets in an oven dish and cover each with a paste made of the anchovies and the salad oil. Sprinkle with peper and cover with the crumbs. Dribble with the melted margarine and bake for 20 minutes in a 375°F. oven.

(*3–4 people*)

7. FISH CAKES

1½ cups cooked flaked fish
¾ cup mashed potato
2 teaspoons chopped parsley
1 dessertspoon hot milk
2 tablespoons chopped fried onion
2 tablespoons oil
Seasoning

Combine the mashed potato, milk, parsley, seasoning, 1 tablespoon oil, fish, and beat till creamy. With floured hands shape small cakes and fry them golden in the rest of the oil.

8. FISH FILLETS WITH BANANA

5–6 fish fillets
Equal number of bananas halved lengthwise
¼ cup seasoned flour
2 tablespoons lemon juice
3 tablespoons margarine
1 tablespoon chopped parsley

Sprinkle the fillets sparcely with lemon juice and then coat them with the seasoned flour. Fry them golden for about 7 minutes in half the margarine and place them on a warm serving dish. Fry the bananas soft but not broken in the rest of the margarine after having rubbed them with lemon juice. Place a half on each fillet and sprinkle with parsley.

(*3–4 people*)

9. Fried Frozen Fish Fillets

8–9 frozen fish fillets
1 cup beer
1 egg
3–4 tablespoons flour
3–4 tablespoons margarine
Seasoning

Beat the egg yolk and gradually add the beer. Just heat, not boil this and pour slowly into the flour, mixing. Add the margarine and seasoning and fold in the stiff eggwhites. Dip the fillets in this batter and fry them in deep oil till golden.
(*4–5 people*)

10. Fish and Potato Pie

1 cup flaked cooked haddock *or* kipper
$\frac{3}{4}$ cup soft mashed potato
2 beaten eggs
3 tablespoons grated cheese
3 tablespoons crushed cornflakes
Seasoning
Margarine

Combine the fish, potato, seasoning, eggs and place the mixture in a greased pie dish. Sprinkle with combined cheese and cornflakes. Dot with margarine and bake for 15–20 minutes in a 350°F. oven.

11. FISH LOAF

3 cups cooked flaked fish
1½ cups soft breadcrumbs
1 cup milk
1 cup top milk
3 small eggs
1½ tablespoons fine chopped onion
½ teaspoon celery salt
Pepper

Combine all the ingredients but the eggs. Add the beaten yolks and fold in the stiffly beaten eggwhites. Place the mixture in a well-greased loaf pan. Set the pan in a tin of hot water and bake for about 1¼ hours in a moderate oven.
(3–4 people)

12. FISH STEW

9–10 small fish pieces
1 cup milk
½ cup water
3 chopped hard eggs
1½ tablespoons flour
½ tablespoons chopped parsley
1 tablespoon margarine or butter
Seasoning

Bring the milk and water to boiling point and add the fish pieces. Lessen the heat and cook the fish for 5 minutes. Add a paste of flour and water and stir briskly till the mixture thickens. Add the margarine, chopped eggs, parsley, seasoning. Serve within a ring of enriched mashed potato.
(4–5 people)

13. Fried Fish

5–6 fish steaks
Batter
Oil *or* margarine

Wipe the fish pieces dry. Dip them all over in the batter and fry fairly slowly in $\frac{1}{4}$ inch depth of oil till golden on both sides.

Batter:
$1\frac{1}{2}$ cups flour
1 tablespoon oil
Water
$2\frac{1}{2}$ teaspoons baking powder
1 teaspoon chopped parsley
$1\frac{1}{4}$ teaspoon dry mustard

Combine the ingredients with enough water to make a batter a little thicker than pancake batter. This is a good batter for fried fish. Without the mustard it can be used for frying certain vegetables.
(*4–5 people*)

14. Oven Fried Fish

4–5 fish steaks
Lemon butter
Breadcrumbs
Seasoning

Dry the steaks and brush them well with lemon butter. Place them in a well oiled pan and bake 20–30 minutes in a 425°F. oven, turning them once.

Lemon Butter:
3 tablespoons margarine or butter
1 tablespoon lemon juice
$1\frac{1}{2}$ teaspoons grated lemon rind
Seasoning

157

Combine and mix until smooth.
(*3–4 people*)

15. BAKED HADDOCK

5–6 haddock pieces
½ cup Ideal milk
½ cup milk
½ cup breadcrumbs
1½ tablespoons margarine
Pepper

Place the haddock pieces in a well greased oven dish and sprinkle with pepper. Pour the Ideal and plain milk over and cover with the breadcrumbs. Dot with margarine and bake about 10 minutes in a 425°F. oven.
(*4–5 people*)

16. HADDOCK KEDGEREE

2 cups cooked flaked haddock
1½ cups cooked rice
½ cup cooked sliced mushrooms
¼ cup Ideal or top milk
3 chopped hard eggs
3 teaspoons chopped parsley
3–4 tablespoons margarine
Seasoning

In a pan melt the margarine and add the rice, fish, mushrooms, eggs, seasoning. Mix well and add the Ideal milk. Simmer a few minutes and place the mixture in a warm serving dish. Sprinkle with parsley.
(*4– people*)

17. HADDOCK WITH NOODLES

1½ cups cooked flaked haddock
1 cup raw small noodles
2 sliced hard eggs
Stock
1 chopped onion
1½ tablespoons margarine
3 teaspoons chopped parsley

In the margarine fry the onion soft and add the noodles. Cook gently for 3–4 minutes and add 2 fingers deep of stock. Boil rather fast, stirring for 5 minutes and then lessen the heat. Add the haddock and heat well. Place the mixture in a warm serving dish and decorate with the egg slices and parsley.
(*3–4 people*)

18. HADDOCK FRITTERS

1½ cups cooked flaked haddock
½ cup milk
2 beaten eggs
2 chopped hard eggs
Oil
3–4 tablespoons flour
2 tablespoons chopped onion
½ tablespoon chopped parsley
2 teaspoons baking powder
¼ teaspoon nutmeg
Seasoning

Sift the flour, baking powder, nutmeg, seasoning, and add the haddock, onion, chopped hard eggs, parsley, and make a well in the centre. Pour in the combined milk, 2 beaten eggs and mix for a loose batter. Drop spoonfuls into hot oil and fry both sides golden. Drain.

19. Haddock or Cod with Herb Stuffing

5–6 pieces cooked haddock or cod
1½ cups sour cream or yoghurt
¾ cup bread and herb stuffing
½ cup chopped onion
1 tablespoon flour
1½ tablespoons margarine melted
1 teaspoon celery salt
Paprika

On a greased oven dish place a layer of combined bread and herb stuffing. Arrange the fish pieces on it. Sprinkle them with celery salt and then cover them with a layer of combined flour, sour cream, onion and melted margarine. Bake 30–40 minutes in a 350°F. oven.
(*4–5 people*)

20. Haddock Tart

Pastry lined pie dish
1 cup cooked flaked haddock
1 cup milk
2–3 sliced hard eggs
3 tablespoons grated cheese
1 tablespoon flour
2 skinned seeded chopped tomatoes
1 chopped onion
3 tablespoons margarine
Cayenne
Salt

In 2 tablespoons margarine fry the onion and tomato soft. Simmer till half dry and spread a layer of it on the pastry. Arrange the egg slices on this. Make a white sauce of the melted 1 tablespoon margarine, flour and milk and add the combined fish, cayenne, salt (very little). Pour this over the egg layer and sprinkle with cheese. Bake golden in a 350°F. oven.
(*4–5 people*)

21. Creamed Kipper

2 boneless kippers
1¼ cups peeled sliced potatoes
½ cup milk
½ cup top milk or cream
¼ cup grated cheddar
2 tablespoons chopped spring onion
1½ tablespoons margarine
¼ teaspoon Basil

Blanch the kippers with boiling water and place them in a flattish greased oven dish. Dot them with margarine and cover them with combined potato and onion. Sprinkle with Basil and pour over the combined milk, cream and cheese. Bake 25–30 minutes in a moderate oven.

22. Mushroom Fish

1 medium tin mushrooms
7–8 small pieces of raw fish
3 lengthwise cut hard eggs
Cheese sauce
½ tablespoon soft margarine
½ tablespoon mayonnaise
½ tablespoon chopped sweet pickles
2 tablespoon grated cheese
Seasoning

Mash the hard yolks and add the mayonnaise, margarine, pickles, and stuff the hollows of the eggwhites with the mixture. Place a layer of the mushroom on the base of a greased oven dish and on it arrange the stuffed egg halves and the seasoned pieces of fish. Cover with the cheese sauce and bake 30–40 minutes in a moderate oven.

Cheese sauce:
To a white sauce add grated cheese and a little made mustard.
(*3–4 people*)

23. Pilchard and Bean Bake

¾ cup soaked, cooked, half mashed beans
1 tin pilchards in tomato sauce
¼ cup bean stock
½ cup milk
¼ cup water
½ tablespoon margarine
1 chopped onion
2 beaten eggs
½ tablespoon flour
2 teaspoons vinegar
Seasoning

Fry the onion and add a thin paste of flour, water, vinegar, stirring till thickened. Add the fish, beans, bean water, seasoning and place the mixture in an oven dish. Combine the beaten eggs, milk and a dash of salt and pour the custard over the mixture. Bake 30–40 minutes in a 325°F oven.
(*3–4 people*)

24. Fish Rolls

¼–½ inch slices raw fish
Chutney
Made mustard
Seasoning

Combine the chutney, mustard, seasoning and spread this paste over each fish slice. Roll them up and fasten with a toothpick. Place on a well greased oven sheet and bake them for about 10 minutes in a 350°F. oven. Serve with a sauce *or* they can be used to fill a pastry lined pie dish and then pouring over them a custard which must be baked till set.

25. PICKLED FISH

2–3 cups small raw fish pieces
1–1½ cups sliced onions
3–4 cups vinegar
7 coriander seeds (optional)
10 whole all spice
½ tablespoon curry powder
1½ tablespoons sugar
1 teaspoon tumeric
Salt

In a pan place the vinegar, onions, sugar, curry powder, tumeric, coriander, allspice and let the mixture simmer till the onions are tender. Salt the fish pieces and fry them till properly cooked and then pack them in jars with alternate layers of fish and the onion slices removed from the vinegar liquid, and finish with a layer of onion. Now pour over all this the boiling hot vinegar liquid, filling the container to the top. Let cool for 12 hours and then close well. This will keep for months.
(*3–4 people*)

26. SARDINE AND POTATO PIE

1 large tin sardines
2 cups thin sliced peeled potatoes
1½ cups milk
2–3 beaten eggs
2 tablespoons melted margarine
1 chopped onion
Cayenne
Salt

Dip the potato slices in melted margarine and place a thin layer of them in an oven dish. Sprinkle it with onion and seasoning and arrange a few sardines on top. Repeat the layers, ending with potato. Pour over a custard made with the eggs, milk and seasoning. Bake 30–40 minutes in a 325°F. oven.

(*3–4 people*)

27. SALMON AND ASPARAGUS BAKE

1 tin flaked pink salmon
½ tin salad cut asparagus
1 cup milk warmed
¼ cup salmon liquid
¼ cup asparagus liquid
1 small chopped onion
2–3 tablespoons flour
½ tablespoon lemon juice
½ tablespoon chopped parsley
½ tablespoon margarine
Paprika
Salt

Fry the onion and sprinkle it with flour, mixing. Gradually add the milk and stir till tickened. Add the combined asparagus and salmon liquids, mixing. Add the lemon juice, parsley and seasoning and after stirring add the salmon and asparagus. If wished this mixture may be topped with uncooked scone shapes and then be baked till they are cooked. *Or* the mixture may be well warmed and served.

(*3–4 people*)

28. Fried Salmon

1 large *or* 2 small salmon steaks
1–2 beaten eggs
Breadcrumbs
¼ cup melted butter
1½ tablespoons oil
1½ tablespoons vinegar
1½ tablespoons stock
½ tablespoon chopped parsley
Seasoning

Place the steak or steaks in a shallow dish and cover with combined oil, vinegar, stock and let stand for 2 hours, basting at times. Then drain the steaks well, dip them into beaten eggs and then into seasoned crumbs. Fry them in melted butter till golden, never letting the pan get dry. Serve with the melted butter and parsley.

29. Shrimp Stew

1½ cups raw or tinned shrimps
1 chopped onion
1 tablespoons oil
1 tablespoon soy sauce
1 tablespoon sherry
¼ tablespoon ginger (optional)
1 teaspoon sugar
Mashed potato
Seasoning

Sprinkle the shrimps with ginger and fry them in oil for a few minutes. Remove the shrimps from the pan and add to it the combined onion. sugar, soy sauce, sherry, seasoning and simmer for a few minutes. Return the shrimps to this sauce and heat well. Serve with mashed potato.

30. Shrimp Fritters

1 cup flaked tinned shrimps
½ cup mashed sardines
½ cup cream cheese
1 beaten egg with 1 teaspoon water
1 tablespoon chopped parsley
2 tablespoons soft breadcrumbs
Seasoned flour
Oil

Combine the shrimp, sardine, cream cheese, breadcrumbs, egg, and with floured hands shape small fritters. Fry them crisp and golden in deep hot fat. Drain them and sprinkle with parsley.

31. Curried Shrimp

1½ cups tinned *or* cooked shrimps
1 cup enriched white sauce
¼ cup sherry
2 tablespoons mushroom or other ketshup
2–3 teaspoons curry powder
Paprika
Salt
Parsley

To the white sauce add the ketshup, sherry, shrimp, seasoning and heat well. Serve on a mound of fluffy hot rice and sprinkle with parsley.
(*3–4 people*)

32. Smoor Snoek

2 cups smoked uncooked dried snoek
1½ cups peeled sliced potatoes
2 large sliced onions
Oil or melted margarine

Soak the snoek for 2-3 hours. Then drain and boil till cooked. Flake and remove all bones. Half boil the onions and then fry them soft. Fry them golden and add the potato and a dash of water. As soon as the potatoes are soft add the fish and simmer gently for a moment or two. Add and toss in a little pepper.
(*4-5 people*)

33. FRIED SOLE

Prepared sole or small soles
Beaten egg
Breadcrumbs
Fried parsley
Flour
Oil
Salt
Pepper

Sift the flour, salt, pepper and rub it thoroughly all over the sole. Then dip it into the beaten egg and cover it with breadcrumbs. Heat the oil and fry the sole, turning it once, till it becomes golden for 10-15 minutes. Drain it, heat it carefully and serve with fried parsley.

34. BAKED SOLE

1 large sole or 2 small ones
$\frac{1}{4}$ cup white wine
$\frac{1}{4}$ cup breadcrumbs
$\frac{1}{4}$ cup melted margarine
2-3 tablespoons chopped onion
2 dessertspoons chopped parsley
Seasoning

In a well-greased flat oven dish place half the onion combined with half the parsley. Place the sole on this and sprinkle with seasoning. Cover with the rest of the onion and parsley and sprinkle with half the margarine. Dribble this with the wine and bake the fish for 20–25 minutes. Now sprinkle with the crumbs and then the rest of the margarine. Grill this golden.

35. GRILLED SOLE

6–7 pieces of sole
1½ cups thin soup
¼ cup sour cream *or* yoghurt
¼ cup brandy
¼ cup grated cheese
1½ tablespoons flour
1 tablespoon melted margarine
1 teaspoon dry mustard
Cayenne
Salt

Poach the fish pieces for about 5 minutes in hot soup. Remove them with a slotted spoon and place them in an oven dish. In a frying pan blend the margarine and flour, mustard. Gradually add the combined hot soup, sour cream, seasoning and stir till thickened. Add half the cheese, stirring till melted and then add the brandy. Pour this sauce over the fish and sprinkle it with the rest of the cheese. Grill till golden.
(*4–5 people*)

36. BAKED SOLES WITH SAUCE

1 large *or* 2 soles
Sauce
¼ cup breadcrumbs
1½ tablespoons lemon juice
1 tablespoon margarine
Salt

In a greased oven dish place the sole and sprinkle it with salt and lemon juice. Bake it for only 5 minutes in a 350°F. oven to stiffen the fish. Then remove it from the oven, pour the sauce over, sprinkle with crumbs, dot with margarine and bake 15–20 minutes till golden.

Sauce:
1½ cups stock *or* milk
    1 tablespoon mushroom ketchup *or* 1 tablespoon Worcester sauce *or* 1 tablespoon capers
1¼ tablespoons flour
Salt
Pepper
1¼ tablespoons margarine

Melt the margarine and add the flour, blending. Gradually add the liquid, stirring till thickened. Then add whichever of the other ingredients desired.

37. SOUP AND FISH BAKE

1 tin undiluted soup
1 tin fish flaked
1 tin drained mushrooms
½ cup grated cheddar
¼ cup fried breadcrumbs
1 tablespoon chopped parsley
1 tablespoon chopped green pepper
Onion *or* garlic salt

Heat the combined soup, flaked fish, mushrooms, green pepper, parsley, cheese, seasoning, and place the mixture in a greased oven dish. Sprinkle with the fried crumbs and bake 20–25 minutes in a 375°F. oven.
(4–5 people)

38. TUNA BAKE

1 tin flaked tuna
1½ cups crushed potato chips
½–¾ cup cream diluted mayonnaise
¼ cup chopped onion
2 chopped hard eggs
1 tablespoon sherry
1 teaspoon capers
2 teaspoons chopped parsley
2 teaspoons chopped celery (optional)
Seasoning

Combine the tuna, egg, onion, capers, parsley, celery, half the potato chips, seasoning. Add the combined mayonnaise and sherry and place the mixture in a greased oven dish. Sprinkle with the rest of the chips, dot with magarine and bake for ½ hour in a moderate oven.

(*3–4 people*)

FISH SAUCE, BATTER, STUFFING, GRAVY, BUTTER

1. Anchovy Fish Sauce

1 cup white sauce
1½ teaspoons anchovy essence *or* paste

Combine and heat the ingredients

2. Black Butter Sauce

2 tablespoons butter
1 teaspoon vinegar
2 teaspoon chopped parsley

Fry the butter till it becomes nut brown. Add the parsley and vinegar and cook 1 minute.

3. Curry Sauce

1½ cups stock
1 skinned chopped tomato
1 small chopped onion
1 tablespoon flour
1½ tablespoons margarine
1 tablespoon curry powder
Salt

Fry the onion soft and add the combined flour, curry powder, salt, stirring well. Gradually add the stock and stir till tickened. Add the tomato and simmer for 15–20 minutes. Strain.

4. EGG SAUCE

1 cup melted butter or margarine
2 hard eggs
1 teaspoon lemon juice
Salt
Pepper

Chop the egg whites and sieve the egg yellows. Heat the butter and add the egg yellow, the egg white, lemon juice, seasoning, mixing, and pour the sauce over the fish or serve it separately.

5. MUSTARD SAUCE

½ cup water
2 tablespoons cream *or* Ideal milk
1 tablespoon margarine
1 tablespoon flour
1 dessertspoon lemon juice
1 teaspoon French mustard
1 teaspoon English mustard
Salt

Melt the margarine and add the seasoned flour, blending. Gradually add the water and stir till thickened. Add the combined lemon juice and the 2 mustards and stir well. Add the cream, stirring it in.

6. SHRIMP SAUCE

1 cup white sauce
½ cup flaked cooked shrimps
1 teaspoon anchovy essence
½ teaspoon lemon juice
Cayenne
Salt

Combine the hot white sauce and the rest of the ingredients and keep warm.

7. FISH BATTER

1 cup flour
Enough water
1 tablespoon oil
2 teaspoons baking powder
1–1½ teaspoons dry mustard
2 teaspoons chopped parsley
Salt

To the ingredients add enough water for a batter a little thicker than pancake batter. This is an excellent recipe that when slowly fried becomes nicely crisp.

8. MUSHROOM AND OLIVE FISH SAUCE

1 cup stock
½ cup cooked sliced mushrooms
¼ cup stoned sliced olives
1½ tablespoons flour
1½ tablespoons margarine
2 tablespoons white wine
Salt

Make a white sauce with melted margarine, flour, stock and salt. Add the mushroom and olives and heat. Remove from the heat and add the wine.

9. FISH STUFFING

1 cup crumbled bread
¼ cup chopped onion
3–4 tablespoons oil
2 teaspoons thyme *or* some other dried herb
Seasoning

Combine the ingredients and use. Other ingredients such as chopped celery, chopped olives, chopped mushrooms and mustard may be used.

10. GREEN GRAVY FOR FISH

3 tablespoons chopped onion
1 tablespoon chopped parsley
½ tablespoon chopped mint
5 tablespoons water
3 tablespoons wine vinegar
1½ tablespoons olive oil
Salt

Combine the ingredients in a bottle. Shake them well and keep in the refrigerator till wanted. Then shake the contents of the bottle well before using.

11. FISH GRAVY

White sauce
1 egg yolk
1 dessertspoon chopped dill pickles
1 tablespoon chopped onion
1 tablespoon cream or Ideal milk
1 dessertspoon chopped parsley
Seasoning

To the white sauce add the onion and parsley. Simmer gently for 5 minutes and add the seasoning. Strain the sauce and add the beaten yolk and cream.

12. Lemon Butter for Fish

2 tablespoons soft butter *or* margarine
1 dessertspoon lemon juice
1 teaspoon grated lemon rind

Combine the ingrdients.

13. Curry Paste for Fish

1 dessertspoon curry powder
1 dessertspoon anchovy paste
1 dessertspoon lemon juice
1½ teaspoon chutney
Pepper

Combine the ingredients.

14. Tangy Dressing for Cold Fish

½ cup salad oil
1 tablespoon horseradish
2–3 tablespoons vinegar
Dash Tabasco
1 teaspoon sugar
½ teaspoon Worcester sauce
Garlic salt to taste

Place the ingredients in a jar and close it tightly. Shake till the contents are well mixed. Can be stored in the refrigerator and must be shaken again before using the dressing.

COOKING TIPS

1. *Bread:* To keep bread fresh sprinkle 1 teaspoon bicarbonate of soda on the bottom of the tin and cover this with a paper napkin.

2. *Cakes:* To grease a tin for baking a cake do not use butter but use Holsum.

3. *Cakes:* Chiffon cakes must be baked in ungreased tins.

4. *Cakes:* Instead of lining a cake tin with greased paper, grease the tin and sprinkle it with equal quantities of flour and sugar. Shake off the surplus after sprinkling.

5. For an angel or sponge cake do not grease the tin. Remove the cake from the tin as soon as it is baked or the sides and bottom will adhere to the tin. The cake top springs back when touched as soon as the cake is properly baked.

6. *Cheese:* To keep cheese from becoming mouldy wrap it in vinegar soaked muslin.

7. *Cheese:* To keep grated cheese while cooking from becoming stringy add a few breadcrumbs to it before cooking starts.

8. *Cheese:* To boil cheese and milk, boil the milk first and then add the cheese. This will prevent curdling.

9. *Cabbage:* To keep cooking cabbage from fading, place a slice of bread over it.

10. *Cream:* To whip cream easily add a pinch of cream of tartar to it or a few drops of lemon juice.

11. *Creaming:* Creaming butter and sugar will be speeded up by adding a few drops of lemon juice.

12. *Custard:* Lumps in wrongly made custard can be removed by beating it with a rotary.

13. *Chocolate:* To make a substitute for chocolate mix $3\frac{1}{2}$ tablespoons of cocoa with half a tablespoon of butter.

14. *Icing Sugar:* To decorate a cake with icing sugar place a lace d'oyley on it and cover the d'oyley with a thin layer of icing sugar. When the d'oyley is removed there will be a pattern of sugar on the cake.

15. *Jelly roll:* After a jelly roll has been baked turn it upside down on a slightly damp cloth sprinkled with castor sugar. Trim off crusts. Then roll up the slab and wrap the cloth around it. Let it cool and then remove the cloth, unroll the slab, spread it with jam and then roll it up again.

16. *Lemon juice:* To keep lemon juice fresh place it in a bottle and add an aspirin. Shake the bottle till the aspirin dissolves and then close it tightly. Keep it in a cool spot.

17. *Nuts:* To remove shells from nuts, soak them in salted water for a few minutes and then crack the nuts gently.

18. *Oranges and Lemons:* If they are kept in hot water for a few minutes before opening and squeezing them they will yield more juice

19. *Onions:* To slice onions without making your eyes water, peel and slice them from the root end.

20. *Onions:* To make onion rings, slice the onions and place the slices in cold water for 10–15 minutes, and then separate the rings.

21. *Onion:* After eating onion chew a sprig of parsley which has been dipped in vinegar and no one will know that you have eaten onion.

22. *Peas:* Do not boil peas in salted water as the salt will loosen the skins.

23. *Peas:* If a few pea pods are added to the water in which peas are boiled they will keep the peas green.

24. *Potatoes:* Potatoes for a salad should be marinated in mayonnaise while they are still hot.

25. *Pudding bake:* Baked puddings should be dusted with fine sugar as soon as they are fully baked and removed from the oven.

26. *Pudding:* It will be easier to boil or steam a pudding if the pudding bag or basin is placed in a colander over the boiling water.

27. *Pears:* Pears used for tarts will gain flavour if sprinkled with a little pepper.

28. *Quicker beans:* If salt is added to the water at once when cooking dried beans they will go a third quicker than otherwise.

29. *Rice:* For boiling rice add a spoonful of lemon juice to the water and it will make the rice whiter and help the grains to separate.

30. *Scorched pastry:* To improve scorched pastry cut off the burnt parts. Then brush the damaged pastry with egg white, sprinkle it with castor sugar and bake it for just a few minutes again in the oven.

31. *Rolled sandwiches:* To make rolled sandwiches easily, remove all the crusts from the bread to be used the day before it is needed. Wrap this prepared loaf in a damp cloth and keep it in a cool spot. Then it will be easy to cut spread, fill and be rolled easily.

32. *Samp:* If gravy or soup is found to be too salty, add a teaspoon of brown sugar and the briny taste will go.

33. *Salad dressing:* If top milk instead of oil is used for salad dressings the result will be almost as good.

34. *Scissors:* Use floured scissors for cutting dried fruit, dates, raisins, candied fruits, etc.

35. *Skum:* If a nut of butter is added to jam as soon as it starts to boil, foam and skum will not appear, and skimming not be necessary.

36. *Tin:* To remove canned food from a tin, punch a small hole in the bottom of the tin and the contents will slip out more easily.

37. *Tin cover:* To remove the tin cover from a glass container holding processed food, thump the container on a firm surface about a dozen times and the cap will screw off more easily.

38. *Tomato slices:* If the slices are dipped into salted and sugared flour before frying, then they will keep their shape.

39. *Vegetables:* Vegetables growing below the ground should be sliced by cutting them from the root end. Those growing above the ground should be sliced from the top down.